T.V. Reddy's
Fleeting Bubbles

An Indian Interpretation

Prof. Ramesh Chandra Mukhopadhyay

Modern History Press
Ann Arbor, MI

T.V. Reddy's Fleeting Bubbles: An Indian Interpretation
Copyright © 2019 by Ramesh Chandra Mukhopadhyay

ISBN 978-1-61599-413-7 paperback
ISBN 978-1-61599-414-4 eBook

Library of Congress Cataloging-in-Publication Data

Names: Mukhopåadhyåaçya, Rameâsa, author. | Vasudeva Reddy, T., 1943- writer
  of supplementary textual content. | Vasudeva Reddy, T., 1943- Fleeting
  bubbles.
Title: T.V. Reddy's fleeting bubbles : an Indian interpretation / by Prof.
  Ramesh Chandra Mukhopadhyay ; foreword by T.V. Reddy.
Description: Ann Arbor, MI : Modern History Press, [2018] | Includes index.
Identifiers: LCCN 2018039083 (print) | LCCN 2018059219 (ebook) | ISBN
  9781615994144 (Kindle, ePub, pdf) | ISBN 9781615994137 (paperback) | ISBN
  9781615994144 (eBook)
Subjects: LCSH: Vasudeva Reddy, T., 1943- Fleeting bubbles.
Classification: LCC PR9499.3.V3743 (ebook) | LCC PR9499.3.V3743 F545 2018
  (print) | DDC 821/.914--dc23
LC record available at https://lccn.loc.gov/2018039083

Modern History Press
5145 Pontiac Trail
Ann Arbor, MI 48105

www.ModernHistoryPress.com
info@ModernHistoryPress.com
Tollfree 888-761-6268
Fax 734-663-6861

Distributed by Ingram Group (USA/CAN/AU), Bertram's Books (UK/EU)

Contents

Foreword by T.V. Reddy iii
Chapter 1: Introduction 1
Chapter 2: The Rural Phase 9
   Women of the Village 10
   The Indian Bride 14
   A Widow 23
   An Old Woman 27
   The Corn Reaper 29
   The House Wife 31
   The Snake Charmer 33
Chapter 3: Urban Phase 37
   Then and Now 37
   Birth Day Party 40
   The Hospital 43
   Let the Eyes Be Shut 50
Chapter 4: Political and Social Phase 53
   'In Exile' & 'Democratic Lines' 54
   The Teacher 58
   My Bare Needs 61
   A Form of Dirge 63
   The Cry 64
   On the Death of Mrs. Indira Gandhi 65
   The Kite 66

When I Churned Time... 69
Chapter 5: Subjective Phase 73
   Agony 79
   Belgium Mirror 81
   'When I Churned Time' and 'Memories' 83
   'My Soul in Exile' and 'A Miracle' 86
Chapter 6: General Phase 89
Chapter 7: Spiritual Phase:- 99
Chapter 8: Conclusion 107
Appendix 1: The Fleeting Bubbles – Complete Text 113
   Foreword by Dr. Georges C. Friedenkraft 113
   Fleeting Bubbles Contents 115
Appendix 2: Reviews of *The Fleeting Bubbles* 151
   Review by A. Russell.. 151
   Review by Dr. Rosemary C. Wilkinson 153
   Review by Prof. Sankarasan Parida 155
   Review by Dr. D.C. Chambial................................. 157
About the Commentator.. 161
About the Author 163
   Other Works by T.V. Reddy 164
Index 165

Foreword by T.V. Reddy

I got acquainted with Dr. Ramesh Chandra Mukhopadhyaya for the first time at the International Poetry Festival 2014 at Guntur in Andhra Pradesh organized by two dedicated devotees of poetry Prof. Gopichand and Prof. Nagasuseela and my acquaintance grew with my admiration for his deep scholarship in English literature and depth in Vedic knowledge. In Feb. 2017, I went to Kolkata on his invitation to give talks for six days on Indian Poetry in English and I can never forget the affectionate hospitality he gave me during my stay for a week in his house. With him I went to all the six places where I gave lectures, four in Kolkata and two in the interior places, and he introduced me to the learned audience before I commenced my speech on Indian English poetry. He is at once a great scholar and powerful poet, a distinguished writer and editor and as such wherever we went, I was extremely happy to see, he was greatly respected and honoured by the audience and the people of Bengal. Moreover as the sole captain of the Underground Literature Movement in Bengal, though he humbly calls him a soldier of the movement, his influence on most of the writers, scholars and the Bengali youth is enormous.

When he expressed his wish to write a critical treatise on one of my poetry books it was a pleasant surprise to me and there cannot be a greater delight than this happy proposal. In January 2017, he commenced the work on my third collection of poems *Fleeting Bubbles* (Chennai, Poets Press India, 1989) which fetched me the Michael Madhusudan Dutt Award in 1994, and after the Sankranti festival in January he wanted to meet me in person so as to get a few clarifications relating to a few of my poems and asked me to give a few talks in Kolkata. To fulfil these two activities I went to Kolkata in Feb.2017 and stayed as his guest in his house on the bank of the river Ganga near Sri Ramakrishna Mission Headquarters. The week that I stayed there in his house was the most fruitful one as we spent most part of the time in literary discussions and discourses that covered both English and ancient classical Indian literature which indeed is the basis for all Indian literatures which includes literature in Indian English too.

The renaissance in India actually started from Bengal, strictly speaking from Kolkata, with the writings of Raja Rammohan Roy, Bankim Chandra Chatterji, Madhusudan Dutt, Swami Vivekananda, Rabindranath Tagore, Sri Aurobindo and others. During my talks in various places in Kolkata and in the interior towns I was introduced to many distinguished scholars and poets in English and Bengali and I could get the opportunity to know about their culture and the contemporary literary trends. Most of them were active members of the Underground Literary Movement which in fact has nothing to do with the generally supposed underground activities usually associated with unlawful activities. In fact it is a dignified body of disciplined scholars and writers intensely humane and humanistic in their thought and heart making an earnest endeavour to spread and strengthen human values in the present society. With unflinching faith in Sanatana Dharma and Vedic values in their original splendour they sincerely make an honest bid to project these values in their writings which have a far-reaching effect on the minds of the reading public. The man behind this mighty humanistic mission is Prof. Ramesh Chandra Mukhopadhyaya, an eminent scholar, writer and social reformer of cotemporary times in Bengal.

As such Prof. Ramesh is the right person to explain and interpret the poems of the book *Fleeting Bubbles* which holds a mirror as it were to the existing social scenario in India. Other scholars may interpret by applying general critical norms which are borrowed mostly from the British and European critical stock and most of them are not aware of Indian poetics and aesthetics and as such they do not feel themselves confident and competent in interpreting and appreciating poems in the light of Indian poetics and theories of Rasa, Alankara, *auchitya, vakrokti* and Dhwani. Most of our Indian scholars still try to draw oxygen of critical concepts for their survival from the almost defunct, worn out and obsolete western theories such as existentialism, archetypal and myth, surrealism, structuralism, post-structuralism, deconstruction, postmodernism etc. woven around the web of narrow confines and time-bound imaginary lines.

While some critics speak of the 'heresy of paraphrase', some others speak of the necessity of 'paraphrasable' content in a poem. In the midst of criss-crossing longitudinal, latitudinal and diagonal lines of critical as well as pedantic jargon justice of acceptable interpretation gets delayed or denied. Most of the scholars and critics in India are totally swayed away by Western poetics with its origin in Aristotle as they are mostly ignorant of or largely prejudiced against the Indian poetics which has its firm roots in the ancient Indian epics, which were written at least two to five millenniums earlier than the Greek and Latin epics. In this context Prof. Ramesh occupies a special place, an unenviable position with his total reliance on Indian poetics while analyzing and interpreting a poem by an Indian poet.

With his thorough knowledge of the Western and Indian poetics as well as the culture of the land and with his toolkit of integrated critical background and approach he can easily open the chambers of the concealed beauties of the poems and make it accessible to the common reader. Many poems abound with cultural connotations, both explicit and implicit, and unless the reader is well-acquainted with the ancient heritage and culture of this country it may not be easy to arrive at a satisfactory understanding of the poems and relish the subtle beauty of the lines. As one goes through this book, the reader can understand better the critical concepts of Dr. Ramesh and the nature of his critical approach in understanding and interpreting a poem.

For easy reference and understanding of the reader the text of *Fleeting Bubbles* and the Critical Reviews that were published are given at the end as Appendix I & II.

T.V. Reddy
Tirupati, Andhra Pradesh, July 2018.

Chapter 1: Introduction

Among all the genres in literature, poetry is the earliest and the most appealing one, and right from the early times it has its sway on the minds of all the people, both literate and illiterate. Thousands of years before the emergence of Greek literature, the earliest epic *The Ramayana* was written in Sanskrit in ancient India by sage Valmiki probably 5000 years before the birth of Christ or by all knowledge even earlier and its appeal is as fresh as it was eons ago in the days of Sri Rama the legendary King of Ayodhya in ancient India and the hero of the immortal epic. About three thousand years before the advent of Christ the second great epic *The Mahabharata* was written in Sanskrit by Vyasa and there is no place or village in India where these two great epics are not read everyday even now. Scholars and historians of the West have totally failed to arrive at the correct date or period of composition of these two great ancient Indian epics thereby misleading generations of readers.

With the passing of millenniums its appeal is growing on the international scene. It is not only a lengthy poem abound with all the literary beauties and flourishes but a permanent work of art and a monument of ethics, aesthetics and human values. That is the reason for its unfading greatness, growing popularity and increasing appeal. In the early times after the advent of Christ, stream of immortal poetry flowed from the quill of Kalidasa the distinguished poet in Sanskrit and while reading his *Sakuntala* the German poet Goethe danced in joy at its poetic beauty that transported him to higher realms. Such is the inspiring spirit and artistic merit of poetry. In the same way in English literature Shakespeare has become an immortal writer with his poetic plays and sonnets of supreme quality. Can we in India forget the unforgettable lines of immortal poets such as Gray, Wordsworth, Shelley or Keats?

To this category belong a few Indian poets in English. In the period before independence Toru Dutt, Sarojini Naidu, Tagore and Sri Aurobindo wrote good poetry judged from any literary or critical standard and their greatness cannot be questioned by any sane or rational reader or critic. All of them come in the long line of Indian poets writing in Indian tradition; language may be English in which they have written, but they are Indians and they never felt that they were away from the land and spirit of India which they projected in their writings. Toru Dutt with her stay with her parents in France and England at the early age imbibed multi-cultural discipline and after returning to India equipped herself with necessary knowledge of ancient Indian epics which enabled her to write some of her best poems on Indian themes.

As a matter of fact Tagore wrote first in Bengali and later translated some of his writings into English. Sarojini Naidu, born and brought up in Hyderabad, was very much influenced by the multi-cultural living conditions, architectural beauty and harmony of the place. The process of thinking was essentially Indian as their minds were steeped in Indian tradition and culture. During her stay in England she was advised by the famous writers of the period Arthur Symons and Edmund Gosse to focus on Indian themes in her poems which she scrupulously followed. With Aurobindo, English was almost his mother tongue as he entered England in his seventh year and after fourteen years soon after the completion of his education he returned to India in 1893. As a matter of fact Aurobindo as a student in London and Cambridge did outshine his British compeers in English and in classics and he scored the highest mark in Greek.

Almost a similar feat was achieved a few years later by Sir C.R. Reddy (kattamanchi Ramalinga Reddy who belonged to the same Chittoor district in Andhra Pradesh from which the present poet T.V. Reddy comes) who outshone the British students as an inspiring orator and he was an outstanding debater and he was the first Indian student to be chosen as Vice President of the Union Society. When he was the Vice President of the Union Society, John Maynard Keynes who later rose to be a world-famous economist was the Secretary of the Union Society. His oratorical skills attracted the natives so much that Members of British parliament requested C.R. Reddy to campaign on their behalf and even as a student in Cambridge, Reddy campaigned on behalf of the Liberal Party in the Parliamentary Elections held in 1906 which swept it into power that year. Many British politicians admired C.R. Reddy's gifts of intellect and eloquence and predicted a great future for him.

When Aurobindo left Baroda College C.R. Reddy succeeded him as the Vice Principal. He later became the founder and the first Vice

Chancellor of Andhra University. While C.R. Reddy shone as an orator Aurobondo shone as a remarkable poet and writer. Though Aurobindo was kept away from the influence of Indian heritage and culture, soon after his arrival to Baroda he earnestly tried to learn Bengali and Sanskrit and succeeded in gaining that knowledge which he was deprived of. Later with redoubled vigour and zeal he presented the glory of our Vedic knowledge. The seed of his voluminous spiritual epic *Savitri* lies in The Mahabharata and it is hailed as a magnificent creation and a wonder in world poetry.

The same cannot be said of the poets who came immediately after the independence. This group of poets is best represented by the anthology of poets edited by R. Parthasarathy i.e. *Ten 20th Century Poets in English*. In these poets there is little of Indian spirit and less of Indian culture. Whenever they made an attempt to refer to Indian mythology or Indian temples they introduced the subject only to subvert their sanctity and significance. Without ever bothering to go deep into the Vedic knowledge and without understanding the truth behind the age-old institutions and traditions and with their half-learned minds they began portraying in a sarcastic vein and indulging in the game of mud-slinging interspersed with glittering laces of irony. It is true the purity of the ancient Vedic knowledge lies beneath the heaps of garbage formed of various narrow creeds and cults over a long period of millenniums going beyond the pages of history.

Is it not the duty of a poet in the real sense to clear a part of this long-accumulated dust? On the other hand most of the so-called renowned poets who manage to shine in the artificial brilliance of Awards are trying to add their contribution of rubbish to the already piled up heap. This is the irony of the present situation of Indian poetry in English. Though many anthologies of poems in Indian English have come out, it is a pity that Parthasarathy's anthology alone, which might have impressed the minds before the Emergency period, is still being prescribed in most of the Universities. It is necessary that professors and scholars are well acquainted with contemporary and recent poets in English and recognize and appreciate the merit wherever it is.

After the period of Emergence, modern poetry in English in its real spirit commences and the poets, fully conscious of the glory of our ancient Indian culture and the present fall of values, have made an earnest attempt in presenting the existing social situation in its real colours. Poets such as Krishna Srinivas, the senior poet from Chennai, I.K. Sharma from Jaipur, I.H. Rizvi from Bareilly, D.H. Kabadi from

Bangalore, T.V. Reddy from Andhra, D.C. Chambial and P.C.K. Prem from H.P., H.S. Bhatia from Punjab, O.P. Arora from Delhi, Margaret Chatterjee and Manas Bakshi from Kolkata, Aju Mukhopadhyaya from Pondicherry, Prof. Syed Ameeruddin and Prof. Radhamani Sarma from Chennai, Arundhati Subramanyam a recent poet from Mumbai and a few others deserve to be mentioned in this context. Krishna Srinivas of Chennai which was familiarly known as Madras had encouraged many younger poets, and some of the senior and well established poets now owe their popularity as poets to him.

T.V. Reddy happens to be one of them and he humbly acknowledges in his talk that it was Dr. Krishna Srinivas, the President of the World Poetry Society Intercontinental, who invited him to the World Congress of Poets held at Madras in 1987 and introduced him to the poets all over the world. Krishna Srinivas dedicated his life to the cause of poetry. And till the end of his life he saw that his international journal *Poet* was alive with the same quality and creative spirit. Of course many new voices have now emerged in the growing field of Indian poetry in English and their relevance can be understood by a careful evaluation of their poetry. But as we go through their poems, most of their writings obviously may fail to stand the litmus test of poetry. Regarding the quality of poetry there cannot be any discrimination based on person or gender or generation.

Observed on the touchstone of literary criticism, T. Vasudeva Reddy or simply T.V. Reddy as he is familiar to the literary world comes out with poetic brilliance. Right from his maiden work *When Grief Rains* (1982) to the recent collection of poems *Sound and Silence* (2017) the poet Reddy has been writing poems with sustained quality and it is indeed a matter of poetic joy to see him writing poems continuously for well over forty years. That he is a born poet is an undeniable fact; he started writing poems as a student in the high School and his poems were published in college magazines in the University. Poetry reading and writing is a passion for him and he undertook the writing of poems both as a joy and as a challenge; that is why he is a careful craftsman always pursuing for perfection. Moreover constant reading and teaching of poetry has equipped him with right poetic diction, and words come to him as naturally as leaves to a plant or tree. It has resulted in spontaneity of expression and nowhere do we feel the poet labouring for expression. Among contemporary poets he is the only poet whose lines run with the natural flow of music, and melody has become an integral part of his poems. And it is a rare gift, a God-given gift indeed.

Though Prof. Reddy has written twelve poetry books so far, for my present purpose I have selected his third book of poems *Fleeting Bubbles*, published in 1989 by Poets Press India, Chennai with the blessings of Dr. Krishna Srinivas who wrote the Foreword to his previous collection *Broken Rhythms* which surprises us with its unbroken rhythmic music. The first five collections till 2005 may form one group comprising the early poetry and the books published from 2008 may be considered for the sake of convenience to come under later poetry though it is very difficult to justify such a kind of division. Though the fifth book *Pensive Memories* was published in 2005, almost all the poems except a couple of poems were written before 2000, but the publication was delayed probably owing to personal reasons although the Foreword was also written earlier. My choice rests on *Fleeting Bubbles* as it is the middle one in the early bunch and even time-wise it comes in the first decade of that block period. Moreover this book, I feel, represents all the features of Reddy's poetry as it deals with the essential elements of Indian life and culture—rural and urban life, political and satirical, social and spiritual aspects.

Man does not learn words by his own self. If a child is pent up in a cave away from human society it will not learn any language. So the impact of influence of life in a group or society plays a greater role in moulding the mind and the expression of a child or grown-up person. Man is always a social animal; all alone away from the society he cannot live and his mind refuses to think of such a solitary life. It holds good to everything connected to the mind and it is equally true in the case of poets, writers and artists such as painters and sculptors. So influence lies in the logic of composing poems and as such intertextuality and anxiety of influence could be espied in the poems of Dr. Reddy who is a wide wanderer both in the golden realms of poetry and in the material realms. And since the signifier as well as the signified of a word is arbitrary, the poetry of Dr. Reddy is loaded with the rich ore of ambiguity. Where is the text? The spirit of the text is not there strictly in the printed material. A text multiplies into as many texts as there are readers and the text of *The Fleeting Bubbles* has been decoded in the light of the present reader's understanding. We allude to reader's aesthetics.

The poet might complain that we have not been able to decode what he had actually thought while writing the poem. But Roland Boucher has rung the death knell of the author in general; and with us the poet of a text is a virtual one or a functional one. To read a poem we must separate it from other poems and to that end a poem has a poet through whom language writes. In other words the poet Dr. Reddy of *The Fleeting Bubbles* is not the flesh and blood poet of Andhra State alone who is a great teacher and profound scholar. And yet ironically enough the virtual poet Reddy and the real person Reddy seem to cross roads. He writes a telling poem on his wife's critical situation that might lead to death. Of course his wife died in the self-same way ten years later and Reddy was flung into a sea of grief expanding into roaring waves of troubles. Poets and prophets are often one and the same.

All of us remember bubbles forged by our saliva hanging on our lips when we were children. We enjoyed with great joy the soap bubbles iridescent with rainbow colours. But they are fleeting and fragile. As children we did not lament for that. Shakespeare said: The earth has bubbles as the water has. And Shakespeare wondered - Whither do they vanish! In fact, whatever we perceive on earth, whatever we experience in life, is transitory as fleeting bubbles. Bubbles also stand for hopes and dreams that are often proved to be myths and moonshine; but however momentary, they have a magic about them. They serve as reminders of the charm and grace or else horrors of the present moment. Does not the poet remind us that whatever we experience in the book of poems must not be taken seriously? We must not be carried away with the experiences embodied in the poems of the book, because they are but fleeting bubbles. Be that as it may, it seems that the readers must be prepared for participating in some harrowing or overwhelmingly pleasant experiences of the poet. But the poet seems to ask us not to take them to heart. They are fleeting bubbles only.

Reading a book of poems is an experience by itself. Some of its imagery sinks deep into the heart of the reader whereas the rest vanish into oblivion, may be for a time only to recur on some unforeseen occasion in the future. In this section what remains left in the heart and mind of the present reader after the perusal of the *Fleeting Bubbles* is being retrieved. The name *Fleeting Bubbles* is itself multidimensional. Countless phenomena show up here in life only to vanish into invisibility after a nanosecond or so. Empirically we do not see the mind. But we perceive our thoughts and feelings popping up and popping out from some inscrutable void as it were. In other words we see the actors and acting, but we do not see the stage where they show up and whence they vanish. No wonder the existence is thus a boundless sea of fleeting bubbles. Every thought is here ephemeral, every feeling and emotion is here ephemeral. Every event is here fleeting, every character is here a shadow; every situation here is a fleeting one. And what we perceive in life is the momentary existence of myriads of things. They come to life in a flash and then they vanish like bubbles in the thin air like the witches in Macbeth. Are we in a charmed world? Or have we tasted the roots that inebriate? Perhaps the title of the collection of the poems *The Fleeting Bubbles* seems to make us aware of this plane of truth.

Chapter 2: The Rural Phase

Most of the poets in Indian English are urban-oriented and as such their poems naturally present the urban life and fail to give us the feel of village life. This deficiency is more conspicuous in the case of the first generation poets after independence right from Nissim Ezekiel and Parthasarathy to Shiv K. Kumar and Keki N. Daruwalla. Even among contemporary poets very few have attempted writing on rural life but with little success. The credit of depicting rural life in its true colours goes entirely to Dr. T.V. Reddy who has successfully filled the hitherto unfilled gap by giving a faithful presentation of village life in India. By presenting the countryside with rural scenes and sounds, situations and events he has brought the rural India into limelight and placed it before the reading community. He stands at a vantage point because he hails from a village, he has his roots in the village, he was born and brought up in the village and even now he lives in the village though it is now nearer to the growing temple town. Since his soul belongs to the erstwhile village he is able to give a faithful picture of village life with all its merits and demerits, joys and sufferings.

As he comes from a marginal farmer's family he knows the rural situation to its roots and understands the problems of small farmers and peasants and the direct impact of the thoughtless schemes of successive Governments on the lives of the small farmers who are now facing acute labour problem and steep shooting of labour charges. He knows the problems of agriculturalists right from the stage of seeding, ploughing, planting, transplanting, weeding, reaping and harvesting. He is a regular participant or witness to almost all the social events of the village such as marriage or festival or function or funeral or some ceremony or ritual. Now he lives for some time in the village and for some time in the nearby pilgrim town and as such he is the proper person to present the realities of both rural and urban lives with his first-hand knowledge and personal experience. His presentation of the rural life is the most reliable and credible one, because he is faithful to his word, unlike our so-called celebrated writers who describe rural scenes by looking through the spectacles of books and journals.

Women of the Village

The opening poem of the *Fleeting Bubbles*, 'Women of the Village', portrays a pale peepal tree by the fast drying pond in a typical village. A banyan tree might live for two thousand years. The oldest peepal tree was planted in 269 BC and it is currently located in Sri Lanka. True, it is quite long a time in the context of the life expectancy of man. But think of the life expectancy of the earth. The scientists say that the earth will be there for another 7.6 billion years. Although life might seem too long for an old man like this author or the poet it is a fleeting bubble in comparison to the life expectancy of the planet earth. And earth is also a fleeting bubble in comparison to the life expectancy of the solar universe. Our solar system is 4.6 giga years old. In five more giga years our solar system would reach the end of its glowing life. Thus nothing lasts and nothing is everlasting. From the micro-organism in the earth to the galaxies in the sky everything and every being dies in a flash and fresh things of their kind are born in a flash like fleeting bubbles.

We are human beings and moreover rational men and women, and as such we are expected to live for hundred years. With us the peepal tree is everlasting. This is why the Hindus praying for longevity chant the mantra:

> Tryambakam yajaamahe
> Sugandhim pustivardhanam
> Urvaarukam iva vandhanaat
> Mrtityormuksiya maa amritaat.

Seated below a peepal tree Lord Krishna avows that He is the *asvattha* among the trees. The implication is clear. That which seems eternal is dying as it were. The *Bhagavad Gita* depicts *asvattha* as the Tree of Life which is deathless. But even the Tree of Life or that which is perennial seems to pale. In other words in the poem 'Women of the Village' we enter into a world where all eternal values are decadent and dying. Here divinity is dying. There is a pond near the pale tree. The waters of a lake or pond stand for consciousness, quietness, mystery and life. The waters cleanse us of our crudities. But here is a pond that is getting dried. Our consciousness is being dulled. Our life force is getting feeble and our serenity is getting scorched. And there the village women come with pitchers for water. The pitcher or the earthen pot, called *kumbha*, is singularly important in Indian culture. We pray to the *kumbha* in the mantra beginning with -

> Kalashasya mukhe Visnuh
> Kantthe Rudrah samaashritah
> Muuley Brahmah
> Kukshau maatriganah sthitah.

In other words all the gods and goddesses reside in the *kalash* or pitcher. The *kalash* should be filled with clean water up to the neck. Then it becomes the container of amrita or nectar. The creator Brahmah carries a *kalash*. Lakshmiji the goddess of wealth and prosperity carries a *kalash*. It is a pity that the womb of prosperity remains starved of water. Our Lakshmis i.e. our women folk in general are being refused the nectar of life and prosperity. Thus we are in a world where life force is on the wane. The pitchers of the deities who live on the abundance of life-force are half empty. They are languishing. It reminds us of T.S. Eliot's *The Waste Land*. It focuses on the barrenness of the land where there is no water but only rock and sandy roads. See how the poem moves majestically with its appealing poetic beauty and pastoral purity:

> Beneath the pale peepal tree
> by the fast drying pond
> in that double roasted hamlet
> women stand like expiring candles.
> Passively they fill
> Their empty earthen pots
> bending like famished cattle
> that drain water to the lees.
> The clear water moves
> In concentric circles
> like their day dreams
> Snaky visages in water.
> Weaving desires in the plaits
> of their cobra-long hair
> they carry pots of sweat;
> Covering their staring breasts
> with their sari-ends
> they turn homeward with pitchers
> and wait for their men
> with flickers in their eyes.   (FB, p.1)

This poem opens with women with empty pitchers at the edge of a fast drying pond beneath a pale peepal tree. Pitchers stand for the womb. Women with empty pitchers speak of a generation where mothers are starved and where the landscape is infertile. When spiritually starved, do we not go to the water bodies for ambrosia and ablution? But alas! The pond is nearly dry, almost empty of water. In other words the women have no source of rejuvenating themselves. The ponds too stand for the womb and they are sterile sans creativity. And the pond is located below a pale tree. In Norse mythology the pale tree is *yggdrasil*, the immense mythical giant ash tree supporting the universe and it is supposed to connect the nine worlds in Norse cosmology. Odin sacrificed himself by hanging himself from this tree; the tree *yggdrasil* could mean the tree of terror. Peepal tree is associated with the tree seated below which Lord Buddha attained his enlightenment. But the tree is now pale. Rays of peace and enlightenment cannot radiate from here anymore, because the waters of the pond are getting dried up. The waters of pure bliss and consciousness are getting sapless.

The women bend like famished cattle to get their pitchers filled with water. This is surrealistic imagery. The women are women and yet they look like famished cattle; the cattle are cattle and yet they look like famished women. It suggests a country where the cattle, too feeble, are also famished dying of hunger. Despite that, down in the very depth of their being they have the lust for life. Their dreams in the waters of their deprived beings show up in concentric circles. Their empty pots touched the drying waters of the pond and stirred them into concentric circles. This tells us how our actions stir our environment and stir our consciousness. Their snaky visages in water are weaving desires in the plaits of their cobra-long hair. The faces of the women are decked with plaited hair. They are stooping at the edge of the pond. To fill their empty pots they push the mouths of the pot into water. The water is stirred into concentric circles. Their faces with plaited hair reflect on the water. The plaited hair and their faces are deconstructed. They look like cobras in kinetic posture. Does it not mean that the tranquillity of the mothers is shattered? They stand for the serpent power or the coiled energy of *kulakundalini* capable of raising revolts fuming in silence.

The action of the poem opens with women with empty pitchers taking water from a drying pond. Their hair and faces reflect on the stirred waters of the pool. They take the waters and carry the pots of sweat homewards. Why do the pots carrying waters resemble pots of sweat? Does it not mean that the mother earth hath strained herself to feed water to her children? The men at home—sons, husbands, and parents are waiting for their daughters, wives and mothers to bring water to them. We can see their starved lips in the thirst-ridden gloom in the shadowy background of the poem as it were. Their thirsting lips cannot speak, but the flicker of their eyes speaks eloquently. The distant homes of the women cannot be descried. But we do very much see the flickers of the eyes of those who are waiting for water from the distance where women are carrying pots of sweat.

The poem is cinematic in its sequence of live shots. Does it not give us a kinaesthetic image of our Mother India? India is as it were a country where desert is fast spreading and intellectual and spiritual decay is writ large where love cannot hold out against the expanding aridity. Does it mean that the land is reduced to such a state where it is not eco-friendly? Are we not responsible for this eco-imbalance? With the gradual deterioration of green cover we are getting deprived of seasonal rains on account of which rivers, lakes, ponds and other water bodies are soon getting dried up. The threat of the land becoming a desert is looming large, isn't it? But we must not take this vignette of village life seriously. The title of the book of poems to which the present poem belongs reminds us such vignettes are but fleeting bubbles. Are they?

The predicament of the poor village women with empty pitchers could only reveal the economic condition of the villages of India. India is a network of villages. And their importance in the economy of the country and in the economic thought cannot be exaggerated. Our best regards to Keynes and Friedmann. But we must be aware of the fact that land or the gift of Nature is the only source of wealth. Earth, water, air, fire and empty space are the only source of wealth. That way agriculture is the most significant economic activity. We have no contempt for industry and commerce. They are the arts that supply the luxuries as well as the necessities of life. The preservation and well being of life certainly depend upon them to a large extent. But they are unproductive in the sense that they produce no extra wealth, because they are gained and not produced. The gains simply speak of the transfer of wealth from agriculture, mining etc to industrial classes. The peasant and the fisherman produce food. He must have a house to live in and clothes to put on. So he hires the service of the artisans. The artisans and industry are thus hirelings of the agriculturists. The artisan draws his incomes as a second hand.

Now where the poor women cannot draw enough clean water from the wells and ponds in the villages, how can one imagine that the agriculturists are well off? What is the factor that ails the rural mothers of the country? They look after the families. And when men and children really starve, when men and children of each family have thirsting lips and when they have lost the power of speech, when they can speak only with the flicker of their eyes do they not liken the boatmen of the poem *Ancient Mariner*? Our country is as it were the cursed boat of the Ancient Mariner where every tongue through utter drought is withered at the root and we can speak no more than if we had been choked with soot. The poem of Dr. Reddy entitled *Women of the Village* provokes a battery of questions in the readers. Are we the rural people of India responsible for our misfortunes? Or is Nature cruel upon us? Is God so miserly with us Indian villagers? Or is the government responsible for the callous negligence of the villages?

The Indian Bride

The scene shifts from a village pond where women gather to get water to a wedding hall. Well the women dipping their pails into the scanty water of a drying pond might belong to the below poverty line or lower class. Women of the below poverty line might sleep with empty stomachs on hard days. The lower class families manage to prevent starvation and they have some roof to shelter them. Then there is the lower middle class and the middle class. The middle class can save for a decent retirement and kid's wedding. Economists might forge such classification on the basis of standard of living. But the economists cannot register the ECG of the pulsating heart pent up in a particular economic parameter. This is left to the poets of Dr. Reddy's stature whose hearts are moved to the reality of the hard-working poor. In the earlier portrait of the lower class village women, it seems that the women are not slaves of their husbands or families. Their desire or the zest for life has been in concrete terms portrayed as weaving plaits of cobra-long hair. This is Pre-Raphaelite art work made of words, created with rich imagination and expertise. Now the words engineer a middle class wedding hall in the poem 'Indian Bride'.

The wedding hall is situated in a temple or a marriage hall. This is significant. Hindu marriage is a sacrament and not a contract. Here a man and a woman are bound for all time to come to the end of *dharma, artha, kama* and *moksha*. That is, as one in unison, they will practice the time-honoured moral laws that hold the society together. Artha and Kama are necessary to existence in the world; one should have the desire to live and without the desire to live existence cannot continue in the world; these two qualities are secular whereas Dharma is a Vedic concept and without Dharma there cannot be any moral order without which there cannot be any peace or joy in the world. The highest virtue Moksha comes in the end and it is the spiritual pursuit. It is related to *Atmagjnana* and *Atma-tattwa* and it is *parampurushartha* i.e. the supreme one among the four. The fruit of Dharma is a lasting one but not an everlasting one, while Moksha is the everlasting fruit. That is why the performance of marriage is a sacred act in Hinduism. Wife and husband will together participate in economic, creative and moral activity. They will participate in sexual act between them for pleasure and procreation. Thus helping each other in physical, mental and spiritual pursuits, they will together strive to get rid of the cycle of birth and rebirth. May be then what Gabriel Rossetti's the Blessed Damozel thought would be real. During the Victorian period in England she spoke to herself -

> We two will lie in the shadow of
> That living mystic tree
> Within whose secret growth the Dove
> Is sometimes felt to be
> While every leaf that His plumes touch
> Saith His Name audibly.

The poem "Indian Bride" focuses on a wedding hall, crowded with well wishers and depicted in minute details. It reminds of the Pre Raphaelite imagery of Dante Gabriel Rossetti:

> Circlewise sit they with bound locks
> And foreheads garlanded
> Into the fine cloth weaving the golden thread
> To fashion the birth robes for them

In the self-same style of word-painting the crowded wedding hall is described by Dr. Reddy. But while Rossetti's imagery generates *santa rasa* or mellifluous peace in the reader's mind, Reddy's portrayal of the wedding hall in all its opulence generates a disturbing feeling or *bibhatsa rasa* in the readers. The temple is overcrowded. The temple environment should generate peace and silence. But here lot of crowd and noise seem to reign; there in the hall there is the concentric circle of friends and vaunting kith and kin. The vaunting kith and kin are only parading their material possessions and attainment. They are not at all drawn to the weal and woe of others. They have no compassion in their heart. This is the foreground of the picture. At the centre the bride and the bridegroom are seated. The bridegroom is winking at the bride just as a beast of prey winks at its game. The bride is elegantly dressed in wedding sari -

> Dressed in gold-laced Kanchi silk sari
> Adorned with stone studded jewellery
> She looks like a bedecked doll in a showcase (p.2)

She is a typical Indian bride, sitting mute and lonely in a noisy overcrowded temple or a spacious marriage hall. The heartless glitter of the wedding party sends a shiver into our heart and there is no mirth and merry-making. Where mirth and merry-making is expected, if we find the vaunting gloom that dehumanizes and the dire hollowness of a ritual is exposed. One wonders whether the much vaunted religious rituals in the name of exploring peace and road to liberation only reveals men as beasts and the bride as a vanishing species in a zoo. But the poet does not stop here simply depicting the scene. He marks the heaving breast, the racing heart and fast breathing of the maiden and knows that emotions of fear are surging in her apparently mannequin figure with greater ferocity than the surging seas. Is not the heart of a woman a sea brimming with love and sympathy? But fear galling the sea of love is not merely the indicator of the anguish mickle; but once the sea is churned with the hurricane of anxiety, if womanhood is stirred by the storms of fear, it might ruin and waylay the whole gamut of human civilization some day. This implicit warning is expressed there.

In the background there are the pale figures of the parents of the bride. Their tears are drowned by the empty show of pomp and pageantry. The readers are apt to ask---What ails the parents of the bride? What ails the bride? In a country like India marching along the road to progress, capitalism has its sway. Money is at the centre of capitalism. If you do not have money you have to starve to death. You will be ravished by ugly devils and your fate is uncertain. In order to protect oneself from the horrors of poverty and starvation one must learn the art of serving the capitalist which is known as education. India is a country where very few men and women are educated enough to serve the capitalist and have a decent living. When men go about unemployed we can guess how helpless the women are, because they are less educated than men even to serve the system. In this context women must serve men who derive income from serving the capitalist. Thus women become slaves of the slaves.

Capitalism is a queer system where there are few free men and everyone is a slave. There are the slaves of the slaves of slaves. And here slavery has to be bought with money. There are gossips in the country that people buy offices with money to earn their livelihood. And no wonder that the womanhood must take refuge with the earning males just as a creeper that survives with the help of another plant and she has to buy her husband. The parents of a daughter must get their daughter married to a man by way paying dowry. They spend all their life-long savings to get their daughter married. Thus prospective husbands sell themselves to their highest bidder. In the market economy the seller has complete possession of the commodity that he sells. Selling transfers the total power over the commodity sold to the buyer.

But this does not hold well in real markets. Because when a buyer possesses a new thing by way of purchase he becomes a slave to it. That is the irony inherent in the market system. You buy a car. You have given it a start every day morning and afternoon. You have to keep it clean. You have to do the servicing to the car and so on. And when the parents spend their life-long savings to buy a husband for their daughter the purchased commodity i.e. the husband becomes the master of the purchaser. That is the paradox inherent in the market system, more so in the matrimonial market. With telling powers, Dr. Reddy describes the predicament generated from this market system where even men are bought and sold:

> Having bought the groom in auction
> As cattle dealers buy their lusty bulls
> She is content to be his slave   (p.2)

By becoming a slave of a free person one could liberate the slave from the pricks of compunctions wrought in him or her. But where is a free person? Thanks to rapid urbanization; the rishis living in forests have vanished like the angels of the mythology. But when we are slaves of slaves we have no security. And hence the heaving heart of the bride -

> Hopes fill her mind like summer showers
> Soon fears settle like monsoon clouds.   (p.2)

One might ask where is the covenant of the buy and sell of husband enacted? The temple or marriage hall here functions as the supermarket. When the buying and the selling in the supermarket called the temple is complete, the buyer i.e. the bride meekly allows the bridegroom who is bought to put on the triple knot or *thali* around her neck. The *thaali* or the *mangalasutra* or necklace with black beads strung from black or yellow thread is prepared with turmeric. According to *Soundarya Lahari* the wife puts on the *mangala sutra* to insure a long life of her husband. Now see into the Hindu ritual of putting on *mangala sutra* in the present day context. When you buy a beast of a man and become its slave to pray for a long life of the beast of a man, there is a travesty of Hindu rituals. And who are the persons that put their seals on the purchase and sale of husbands in the temple? They are the priests only. The *Purohit* performs the rites of buying and selling by Agni. To buy the husband for their daughter the bride's parents must have borrowed money. And the poet sees the borrowed currency in flames. Is it not economics of waste innovated by civilization? Does it not remind us of the Fire Sermon of Gautama Buddha? -

> "Oh you seekers of Truth, mark that everything is burning. The eyes are burning, senses are burning, thoughts are burning...."

Dr. Reddy in his wonderful poem "The Indian Bride" has shown how the dowry system is not merely a freak; it is very much a part of the capitalist system that rules the day. Here men and women have been turned into commodities. They have been dehumanized. The market system has transformed them into beasts. The power of capitalism has sway over every institution. It has appropriated time-honoured traditions as its own. Even religion functions as the handmaid of capitalism. We are told that change is the category of life. Nothing lingers beyond tomorrow. The poet wonders whether the shape of things prevalent in the capitalist system is a painful reflection of fleeting bubbles!

As a matter of fact the poem 'The Indian Bride' opens with the three lines which succeed in creating the necessary atmosphere:

> Amid vaunting faces of kith and kin
> Concentric circles of friends
> She is alone in solitude   (FB, p.2)

Now let us look into the sound system of these three lines. M of amid, *n* of vaunting, *n* of kin, the two *n*s of concentric and the *n* of friends, *n* of alone, *n* of in,—all these *m*s and *n*s are nasal sounds. They are as it were being suppressed by the voiced '*v*' of vaunting. The voiced labial fricative is as it were robbed of its force under the impact of the unvoiced labial fricative *f*. While the *m* and *n* give us a suppressed moaning sound it is being further suppressed by the voiced *v* which is rather loud and vivacious. But its effervescence pales beside the unvoiced fricative *f* which seems to stammer. Then with the velar '*k*' in kith and kin and *k* sound in the words concentric and circle the sound is brought down to the ground level which has nothing spectacular about it. And finally the whistling sound of '*sh*' in she, '*s*' in faces, circles, friends and solitude suggest the sound of hushed weeping that has no ending because *s* is no stop consonant.

Now let us look at the word picture. A lady sitting alone is at the centre of concentric circle of friends and kith and kin vaunting. Does it not look like a paradox? A lady does not sit surrounded by foes. She is surrounded by her friends and relatives. While others are plunged in merriment and vaunting or praising her excessively, she remains alone. She does not participate in the merry-making. It is a wonderful montage. The vaunting of the surrounding friends and relatives emphasizes the sadness lurking in the lonely lady. The poem seeks to decode the paradox inherent in the scene. The lady is sitting by her groom and the groom is also silent. He is winking at the surroundings. He does not seem to be depressed. But he is not surrounded by his friends. He along with his bride sits surrounded by the friends and relatives of the bride. How does the lady look? She looks like a mute adorned idol in an overcrowded temple. The imagery is significant. Conversely it suggests that the idols remain mute in a temple despite our vaunting. And one wonders whether these idols feel lonely encircled by the vaunting crowd.

The poet feels that he has not been able to describe the lady before the readers to his fill. So he goes for another simile. Clad in a gold laced Kanchi silk and decked in stone-studded jewellery she looks like a doll. They are not ordinary stones; they are in fact chiselled pieces of precious stones of great value. Moreover sari is not an ordinary cloth, it is made of special silk prepared at the famous city Kanchipuram or Kanchi. It is an age-old fashion to buy silk saris woven at Kanchi for special occasions like marriage in South India and the bride is seen wearing invariably Kanchi silk sari which is a costly one. Stones add to her figure a solidity of an inanimate image. The lady does not look like a human being. She looks like a doll. She has no will of her own as it were. She is not a lady pulsating with life. What robs her of her humanity and joy in life?

But Reddy has not finished with the description of the lady. She is as it were a vanishing species in a zoo. Mark you the world is a zoo where women are treated as animals as it were. Reddy imagines that the rise and fall of the waves of the Bay of Bengal even when tossed by gales pale before the heaving breast of the lady. She must share the spikes and dips of her unknown fate in the tracing of life with an unseen face. Beneath the pomp and glitter of the marriage party loud with mirth, flows the unimpeded flow of tears of her parents. The priest or the Indian *purohit* observes *homa* by lighting the sacrificial fire. They are supposed to pray to gods with all their hearts so that the newly married couple is blessed.

But what they do actually is to pour ghee into fire, but in this context it is invested with the symbolical meaning of pouring or throwing borrowed money into fire. Yes, the parents of a bride have to borrow money often to get their daughters married. At the same time the vast investment to insure the happiness of the daughter--- the feasting of friends and relatives, the religious rituals, the greetings to one another and the high hopes—turns into ashes! Why should they borrow? They are compelled to borrow because the dowry system exists here in India. You have to buy the ox of a bridegroom for your daughter with dowry and paradoxically enough your daughter becomes a slave to the caprices of the ox! The three knots of the *thali* or *mangala sutra* around the neck of the bride do not mean the union of the bride and bridegroom on three levels---spiritual, mental and physical. The *mangal sutra* turns into a shackle around the neck of the bride henceforth. She is thrice cursed as it were and is hurled headlong with hideous ruin and combustion down to lifelong perdition flaming from the ethereal sky of parental love.

Thus the poem is a sharp shaft of satire shot against the marriage ritual in India. In India the woman does not have the opportunity to know the man and they do not know each other before they meet at the wedding. The poet seems to pooh-pooh such customs. But are marriages in other societies with different customs always happy and successful? The dowry system in India is very cruel indeed. But why should they pay dowry? The more well-placed is the bridegroom, the richer the bridegroom, the higher the amount of dowry to be given to him. This is an offshoot of the capitalist system. Hope for material prosperity of the bride in times to come impels the parents to pay dowry to get their daughters married. Here material considerations are more and the pious wishes for the children are less. God is a mute witness to such events. The image of the god likens a doll. It has no will of its own as it were. God is used as a doll to serve the desires of man on such occasions.

Aristotle tells us of three ways of persuasion - ethos, pathos and logos. The poet here employs pathos—an appeal to emotion to convince the readers through the word painting of the bride and bridegroom surrounded by the well wishers amidst glitter and apparent gladness. In the first half of the poem the poet creates a natural picture instead of describing the situation or telling and as such the poem is more dramatic; in the second half both showing and telling combine. The poem however by way of describing an Indian wedding seems to strike a deeper import. Behind the apparent glitter and glow of the phenomenal world there is a well of sorrow. The poem reminds us that the life and world is full of sorrow despite the fact that they look otherwise. Futility lurks behind every effort of man to get at pleasure and happiness.

May be, each one of us is a bride. Every self that is born is a bride. And as soon as the self is born it is wedded to the world or non-self whom the self has not seen earlier. The self toils hard to buy the non-self for its own pleasure. But once we buy a thing for our pleasure we become its slave. We have seen this in the instance of a car. We buy a car for our comfort and we have to see that it starts every morning and evening.

The village in the poem 'Women of the Village' could stand for the whole country of India. The 2011 census of India states that 68. 84 percent of Indians live in villages. The profile of Indian villages is the real profile of India and surely women are its backbone. And see what *Manusmriti* observes:

> *Yatra naaryastu pujyate ramante tutatra devataa*
> *Yatra etahstu na pujyate sarvahstatra aphalah kriyaa.*

It means the gods do reside in the place where women are praised and honoured. Every activity in a society is in vain and fruitless where women are ignored. The Atharva Veda 12.1.26 prays—'Oh Motherland! Give us the aura that is present in girls.' And one wonders what men in India have made of woman. In this context let us see the state of an Indian bride.

The Indian bride buys a husband only to be his slave. This is directly related to the dowry system prevalent in India. Dowry is the euphemism for the money paid to get a husband. But this is not Indian tradition. In the pre-colonial India there was no dowry system. When money or inheritance is given to a groom's family by the bride's family it is dowry. But in India when marriage ceremony takes place the parents and the relatives of the bride's family transfer wealth to the bride and mind you they belong to the bride only. So dowry in the right sense of the term was not usually practiced in pre-colonial India. Rather it was associated with Gift Economics. But now see the existing situation and scan the scene:

> Having bought the groom in auction
> As cattle dealers buy their lusty bulls
> She is content to be his slave.   (FB, p.2)

This is true in the contingent. This is the usual practice in marriages in India. After marriage she has to work in the field. She has to bring up the child. At home she is flogged by her drunken husband. This is a sharp criticism of the market system. When could buying and selling take place in the market? It is assumed that the seller has total power over the commodity she or he sells. When the sale deed is complete the seller relinquishes all the power over the commodity sold and the total power over the commodity is transferred to the buyer. In other words a market is only possible when both the buyer and seller are free men capable of possession of what they possess or relinquish. But it is not so here. This meaning of buying and selling no longer holds in this context. The buyer becomes the slave of the commodity he or she buys. One buys a car and he becomes a slave of the car. One buys a flat and he becomes a slave of it.

Even people here buy offices and employments in exchange for money. Alice was in wonderland while we are in a blunder-land. Here we do not buy commodities. Commodities buy us instead. Thus through a parable of marriage ceremony Dr. Reddy exposes the market system. Economics is concerned with the production of wealth and distribution of wealth. In modern world market is the only channel through which distribution of wealth is possible. But earlier reciprocity and gift were also channels for the distribution of wealth. When other channels for distribution of wealth are struck down market system also cannot survive for long.

There are village fairs or weekly markets in villages where cattle are bought and sold. Men become cattle sold to the highest bidder. In short they are dehumanized impelled by their inherent greed for money. Being bought they possess the buyer herself. This is due to the internalization of the patriarchal system by the womanhood of the country. Thus, only economic motives do not operate in the market. Economic motives are controlled by extra-economic forces. This is a remarkable piece of a poem that involves socio-economic considerations as well as cultural matters. It is at once mind-stirring and thought-provoking with its multi-layered thought pattern.

A Widow

The heart of the bride at the wedding party beats terribly fast, for no one knows what awaits her in the future. In this context when poor women become widows they are looked upon as ill omen. Often even a widow's children try to avoid her presence especially on auspicious occasions. But is this the traditional view? Note. King Dasaratha died leaving three widows. One does not find any disrespect for them anywhere in *The Ramayana*. They are not alienated from the family or the society. Tara remarries. Besides a widow could have children by *niyoga*. If the widow chooses an austere life she is revered just as we revere an ascetic. But one is apt to ask--What caused the devaluation of widows in our society? That needs a long discussion. But suffice it for the time that disrespect for widows is not traditional in Hindu society. It is a pity that while men look upon widows as evil omen nowadays they want to enjoy her flesh secretly:

> Still her glimpse even in a mirror
> Transports them to heights of pleasure.   (FB, p.20)

This exposes the men in our land who are plunged in *tamasik* way of life and thinking. *Tamas* is related to darkness and it seeks to hide evil designs and dark deeds and things. There is no straightforwardness in our countrymen. There are many poets who lament the plight of widows today in India. But the message of Dr. Reddy is different. He laments the tamasik attitude among us Indians. We do not have the courage to assert in public what we feel in private.

One wonders whether India is the land of Buddha the Enlightened One. In order that one could meditate on the sorrows of man one needs a conducive environment. Lord Buddha meditated under the peepal tree and attained enlightenment. But now the peepal trees are withering. And look at the band of Sujatas. The women stand like expiring candles on the edge of a drying pond. The imagery of candles reminds us of Lord Buddha. Lord Buddha does not believe in substance. So he does not pin his faith on individual soul. But he says instead of the soul our desires are reborn. Desire or *tanha* is the flame. The body functions as the body of the candle. According to Lord Buddha when the candle or the flame in the candle extinguishes one gets rid of the birth and rebirth cycle and attains bliss or nirvana.

But Dr. Reddy posits that these village women have never dared to have desires and sans the joys of living they are like expiring candles. This is the visual representation of death in life. Dr. Reddy reminds us that extinction of desire is not always bliss or nirvana. It is better to have desires than to have no desire at all. The women in rural India are passive like famished cattle. And lo! In a flash they look like cobras with their plaited hair or intricately woven desire of the subconscious and unconscious. The waters of the drying pool function as the magic mirror that detects the desires lying hidden in them. The poem itself could be read here as the magic mirror.

We have seen how husbands or masters are bought in exchange of money. Yes this is not the case only in relation to marriage in India. People often buy their employment in exchange of money. In other words people buy their servitude; because this is a queer world where unless you are a slave you have no identity. Are you a professor? No? Are you an engineer? No? Are you a married lady? Then what are you? You have no identity. You do not exist. That is the way of the world here in India. We have already witnessed the chilling pomp and pageantry of a wedding party. The lady thus married could be a widow. As per the census department the population of India during 2011 was 121 crores and of this 5.6 crores were widowed; and what could be their predicament? Dr. Reddy pens their exact plight in telling imagery.

In fact this is where we could invoke Levi Strauss. There are only differences and no positive terms in language. And kinship could be read in the light of structuralist interpretation of language. There is no substance in widowhood; it is a human construct. But curiously enough men look upon their own constructs as something ordained by extra human powers. This is impelled by their materialistic values. Think of a widow who has no power to earn. Should we not stand by her? Our utilitarianism, our propensity to acquire more and to spend less for others goes against our innate human nature. But alas! We go against our nature and dub the helpless widow as evil; thereby we have an excuse for ignoring the widows and the poor. How do we look upon a helpless widow? Look at the photographic presentation of the widow:

> Her very sight is a sore to the mind
> She is shunned as a viper
> As if she is a castaway leper. (p.20)

Should we hate a leper? Should we cast away a leper? Everybody will say 'no'. But it is a pity that when we see a leper on the roadside we avoid him or her. In the selfsame way we shun a widow. Leprosy is not always infectious; but some form of leprosy could be infectious. Even if it is infectious the society should look after the welfare of a leper. But see the state of a widow. Why is she cast away? The only reason is that she becomes a liability for the society from economic point of view. Money spent for the poor and the disabled will impoverish the society. This takes the wheel of time back to ancient Sparta where the old and helpless were killed. But unlike ancient Sparta we do not have the guts to say that. On the contrary if we posit that the poor and the helpless women are evil we can easily kill them or starve them to death and that is being practiced. May be this attitude has been generated by Calvinism a harbinger of capitalism. Calvinism posited that the rich are blessed. Had they not been blessed how could they make money and attain prosperity? And if the wealthy man is God's elect, must we not hate and avoid the poor?

> They feel her quaint breath
> Puts out prospect or success   (p.20)

It is a curious imagery. Every man is as it were a ceramic vase. Inside him the lamp of future prospects and hopes for success in the ventures of life burns. Are such hopes and thoughts of prospects rational? But ironically enough we men have shaped science tarnished by our irrational desires. And we forged such disciplines as statistics to foresee the shape of things to come. Now they believe that the breath of the widows might put out the lamp of prospects in them. Quite funny! However much our science may have developed, superstition has influenced our attitude; we are sorry!

We are turned against our innate love for men and fellow feeling. But curiously enough, thanks to their unscientific science, while instinctively they do often recoil from a widow, they are never short of words regarding how to lift up the fortunes of widows and desolate women. Who would lend them attentive ears? Only foxes and asses would lend their ears. In other words men, if any in the right sense of the term, are few, very few. Majority of men are foxes and asses in human flesh. But see, the very people who seek to avoid the very breath of a widow, because it could bring misfortune upon them, yet talk of their plans to change the fortunes of the hapless and they do not shudder to imagine that these widows could gratify their lust. They are full of greed to take advantage of the hapless women. Their heads are full of the faces of those hapless women. A widow's glimpse in a mirror could transport them to untold pleasure.

According to Tod, Alauddin Khilji saw the beauty of Padmini on the mirror and was infatuated with her. Those who are transported to pleasure seeing the faces of the helpless widows are no doubt Alauddins sans empire and courage. There are so many Alauddins among the males in the country. And yet the propensity to avoid the helpless and the widow has taken such shape in our mind that it has been a taboo to see a widow in any auspicious ceremony. Even the son of a widow fears to look at his mother lest his marriage fails. Thus what the economists do not care to notice, and what the anthropologists do not perceive is left for the poet Reddy to delineate. Margin is at the centre of centre and the poets are also drawn to the margin and to marginal women such as the widows.

Among the many occupations in the society that of the hunter is most cruel. When he kills a dove, clips its wings and thrusts it in the bag he strikes fear into our hearts. Because normally we look upon one who kills living things as cruel. They are not supposed to be scared of anything. But even the hunter shrinks at the sight of the forlorn widow. The imagery is significant. There might be no objective reason to fear and yet we are scared of helpless men, things and situations. Thus fear is often subjective and a gift of collective imagination.

It is evident from the poem that in order that the rich people and ruling class want to be at the centre of the society they earmark the poor and the helpless and the women as evil. If some people are not identified as evil how could the ruling and the rich become honourable. If there were no darkness how could there be the light? So those who want to remain in the lime light must banish some of their weaker fellowmen to darkness. The widow in India has been forced to live in this man-made darkness. She is as it were a denizen of the borderland of the human world. We look upon her with awe and fear.

Helpless widows in general, we have observed, thrown away from their families, often take refuge in the neighbourhood of a temple. Temples and churches have ever been the shelter of the weak and the poor. Totally helpless widows thrown away from their families, mostly from Uttar Pradesh, W.Bengal and Odisha, often come to Brindavan and take refuge. Brindavan is a temple-crammed city where thousands of Bengalee widows (40,000 or so) crowd as beggars. In fact abandoned by the family, deprived of any means of livelihood, where should people go but to temples and seek refuge with God? No outfit of revolutionaries can deliver them goods. They do not have the communes where they can give shelter to the widows and arm them against the odds of the capitalist society. The Supreme Court decreed the Maintenance and Welfare of Parents and Senior Citizens Act 2007. But the widows are not aware of the law. Besides they cannot afford to assert their rights at the court. So helpless against the savage atrocity of the capitalist system that teaches us to satisfy our cravings even at the cost of our near and dear ones, the widows take shelter in the neighbourhood of the temples.

An Old Woman

Reddy's poem 'An Old Woman' opens with such a helpless woman addressing the pilgrims in the neighbourhood of a temple:

> 'Please give me alms, O charitable one!
> I am an old woman with help from none' (p.21)

These beggars have a function in the society. It is true, that every man is brimming with desires. And one of those desires is the desire to give. (Economics however is indifferent to man's desire to give without anything in return.) These beggar women appeal to the pilgrim's desire to give. The old woman's voice in the vicinage of the temple is a familiar one to the poet. The poet gives a vivid portrayal of the old lady:

> Her hair as gloomily grey as clusters of snakes
> unkempt, uncombed and untouched by oil
> Her nails often scratched her scalp
> and brutally killed the lice that lived there long ...
> (p.20)

Her bare arms were loaded with blisters. Her breasts and face and brow were all wrinkles. Her sari had more stitches than the countless wrinkles in her body. Her eyes were weak. She could not move without a stick. Unlike the rest of the mankind she did not have any other desire than to have her stomach filled with grub. And her only prayer was to be visited by Death. Plunged into longing for death, she was indifferent to people looking at her.

This is a powerful word-painting of Thanatos or death-wish. One wonders whether she is the image or incarnation of our motherland India, a developing country, groveling in distress and darkness of material and spiritual poverty. But God is pent up in the temple. He cannot come out of the temple to rescue his devotees. God cannot even grant death to those who suffer death in life in this country. Although Indian spiritualism posits that God is everywhere especially in the poor and the destitute, the priests who stand for Indian spiritualism curse the destitute.

> The Swamiji saw her on his way, spat at her
> and went in fury for his ill luck to see her first. (p.21)

In a flash the attitude of the Indian Swamis is brought to foreground. Although we expect the Indian Swamis overflowing with the milk of human kindness they are just the opposite of what we expect of them. The great poet Sankaracharya warned us in his *Charpata Panjarika Stotram* which is familiarly known as Bhaja Govindam:

> Jatilo mundi lunchita keshah
> Kaashaayambara bahukrita veshah
> Pasyannapi cha na pasyati mudhah
> Hyudaranimittam bahukritaveshah.

This memorable *sloka* can be translated in the following words:

> Men with matted hair, men with shaven heads,
> Men in saffron robes, men in many a guise—
> Fools have eyes to see, yet they do not see
> All these roles and guises donned to fill their bellies.

The reader might ask—how did the old lady react to the spitting at her by the temple priest? She was just indifferent to the antics of the Swami. The omniscient narrator answers:

> Long back she resolved to have neither eyes nor ears
> She sat on the hard but hospitable stone for decades
> A statue of tolerance fed on hard ignominy
> A haunting figure with a soul wrung in agony. (p.21)

There has been no better description of such metamorphosis of human body hurt with grief. People are stunned into stone in agony. Do we not find the image of our motherland in the image of the old lady? Where is God to rescue us from the distressing situation? God, if any, has also resolved to have neither eyes to see nor ears to hear. Both the old woman and God have chosen to become statues of tolerance even though their hearts bleed. Both of them have opted for stones as their seats. Stones are more comfortable than snug and secure cots with in well-decorated houses.

The poem not only focuses on the state of Indian womanhood, it also exposes the vanity fair of the temple institution and the institution of the Swamis. More often temple priests have become almost money-collection agents and cashiers eager to count all the currency notes and coins of varied denominations offered to the idol by pilgrims and devotees in the *harathi* plate and in the *hundi* which is the safe container to hold in its womb all the money gently pushed into it by the devotees. The poem is a harsh reminder of the commercial bent of mind of purohits or the temple priests and swamis of the modern times. Though they are expected to serve the poor and the needy and the destitute they ignore their basic obligations and moral principles by becoming the worshippers of Mammon and look at the poor with contempt. The poem is time and again in its ruthless realism that down razes all our emotions for the establishment.

Literature made of words moves in time while painting manifests itself in space. Dr. Reddy is one of those rare masons working with words whose poetry made of words is clinched up in spatial imagery. Look at the closing lines of the poem quoted above –'A statue of tolerance fed on harsh ignominy'. What a surpassingly beautiful image! It is this spark of spontaneity that elevates his poetry to the level of the immortal classical poets in English. Thus the old woman who belongs to a particular time and space becomes timeless –a symbol of the Mother Earth. The statue reminds us of Michel Angelo's portrait wrung in agony.

The Corn Reaper

The scene now shifts to the paddy field. The sight of a paddy field full of ripe crops bathes us in fine excess. And when a solitary reaper cuts and binds grain and sings, it is the sight and sound for gods to see and hear. What Wordsworth did not notice in the cold country Reddy observes in a hot country like India. Here the reaper labours in the Sun with a multi-toothed sickle. Sweat flows from her brow in drops. So, that is the figure of a reaper in a ripened paddy field. Wordsworth in his Solitary Reaper does not dwell on how she looks, nor is his mind drawn to the state of her life and her struggle for existence except a vague verbal hint of some natural sorrow or loss of pain. Obviously all the stress is on the musical note; but in Reddy's poem stress is on the existential predicament and the bitter realities of life. Wordsworth is the poet of the ear, but Reddy is the poet of the eye and the heart. Unlike Wordsworth, Reddy gives us a vivid picture of her appearance:

> Under the scorching sun
> in the ripened paddy field
> she reaped the fallen crop
> with the multi-toothed sickle,
> sweat flowed drop by drop
> from her care-worn brow;   (p.22)

When the song of the reaper is heard no more, Wordsworth the poet of the ear carries the song of the solitary reaper in his heart. But Reddy is drawn to her hardship. Reddy pen-pictures the quandary she faces. She is solitary because she does not pay heed to whether anyone looks upon her. She reaps the fallen crop with the sickle with all attention. But lo! She is not all alone. The landlord's greedy eyes are on her heaving breast. Any moment the rich and the powerful can abuse a flower by force. Unaware of the landlord she cuts the corn patiently sitting like a flower. A flower that blossoms stands as a symbol for its chaste beauty and bliss. But she is being eaten at her heart by her thoughts of the wailing child at home. She is a beautiful maiden whose heart is laden with sorrow eager to caress her child who is away. A closer analysis of the poems of the two leads to the conclusion that while Wordsworth's poem appeals to the mind, Reddy's poem appeals to the heart.

She is not physically fit to work hard because of the volley of the blows on her back yester night. Surely her drunken husband will repeat the same action when she returns home after the whole day's bone-breaking labour. So fear also silently works in the flower of the maiden. Thus here is a reaper of a woman whose aching body cuts and binds the grain being fully engrossed. She is not apprehensive of the possible dangers around her. From a distance the gormandizing landlord looks upon her. Though immersed in work she cannot forget her child who cries at home. And she knows that on her return home a thrashing awaits her from her drunken husband. Thus a working woman in the field is a mournful image of unbearable sorrow struck by fear. And she has to bear it.

The poem is a dramatic lyric. It describes a woman in a breath-taking situation. Beasts of men surround her, but she cannot flee. She takes care of herself and she must take care of the wailing child! Perhaps Harold Bloom's anxiety of influence does not work in this poem. An eye for minor details and a truthful voice here portrays the situation of a reaper in the Indian paddy field which is exactly the opposite of the portrait of the solitary reaper whom Wordsworth saw and heard. While Wordsworth did not take into cognizance the objective situation of the solitary reaper, Reddy takes care to note that. This difference is all the more important, because it is this that distinguishes Reddy the modern poet from the Romantic poet Wordsworth; while the romantic is carried away by the external sound of the song, this Indian rural poet looks into her heart and her inner feelings as a humanist. He does not belong to the Romantic Period of England after all. Yet he creates a sweet lyrical song that tells us of the woman's sad life and saddest thoughts. After all, long back Shelley said in his memorable poem 'To a Skylark' - 'Our sweetest songs are those that tell of saddest thought'.

The House Wife

We have seen women going to the drying pond to fetch water. We have seen a woman in marriage party. We have seen a widow. We have seen an old woman begging in the vicinity of a temple and a young rustic woman reaping the corn in the scorching sun to make both ends meet. All these poems portray woman from various angles purely from the realistic point of view without giving any scope for peregrinations of imagination or falsification. Now the poet shifts to another role of a woman viz. that of a housewife.

The poem opens with the sullen Sun descending behind the western hills. The expression sullen sun is an instance of transferred epithet. Who is sullen? We have to wait for the answer. If someone is sullen the environment becomes queasy. The land under the sullen sun is harshly bright, hot and humid. Dusk, waiting like a prowling wolf or the prowling devil seeking someone to devour, leaps and swallows up the valley. In other words the whole valley with its surrounding hills all of a sudden vanishes into indeterminate darkness. In this all pervading darkness black crows, a peepal tree, thatched hut, walled with mud, are vaguely discernible. It is as vivid a portrayal of the villages in Central and South India as Hardy's description of the Wessex region in his great novels. Crows are black. In the pervading darkness the black crows are espied. Weary with their bootless flying they settle on the withering bough of the peepal tree. The flutter of the wings only enhances the eerie silence of the boundless darkness. The drying peepal tree is the sentinel of the village. The entrance of many of the villages in India is indicated by a big tree like peepal. The withering boughs of the peepal tree only suggest that the village one enters is gloomy and glum. The tree stands silhouetted in darkness with crows resting on its branches. Thatched huts and walls of mud could be guessed in the darkness:

> Thatched huts and walls of mud stand
> the living symbols of their lifeless life;
> the huge clay barrels, all empty,
> emit a hollow sullen somber smile
> at the searching eyes of the housewife   (p.23)

And in the all pervading darkness a sudden light of the clay lamp reveals the huge clay barrels all empty. The light of the clay lamp draws our attention to one hut among the many huts. The housewife lights a lamp hesitatingly with the twig of a plant. She hesitatingly burns the lamp because she has not enough fuel to burn. The light of the lamp reveals the empty barrels and the empty barrels laugh at her. She waits for her husband to turn up after the whole day's bone-breaking labour in the field:

> She lights the clay lamp
> with a burning twig
> and waits with a wick in her eyes
> for her partner from the furrowed field.   (p.23)

She is hungry. May be she did not have any food the whole day. But hope springs eternal in human breast. And she feeds her empty stomach with hopes although she has none. This indeed is the real picture in most of the huts of the poor of below poverty line in the villages of Rayalaseema, the region which is a part of Andhra State to which the poet belongs. Their well known concept is - Unless hands work hungry stomach cannot be filled. This is direct reference to the poor peasants who work from dawn to dusk in contemporary India. The present reader wonders whether the hut we live in called India has a blank future. Does Mother India starve with her millions of children? There is fuel crunch for millions. The housewife puts off the lamp to save fuel. But the wick of her eyes alighted by the lamp and by the hoping against hope lingers. A picture of a maiden's eye with a flicker is clearly and distinctly perceived by the readers amidst encircling gloom. Is that the wistful eye of our mother, Mother India? Poetry is in pity here and pity is pregnant in the stark reality reflected in Reddy's poetry.

The Snake Charmer

Dr. Reddy focuses on the different occupations in the poorer rung of the society. He has touched upon the corn reaper. He dwells on the hunter. He tells us that even a hunter who clips the wings of a dove and thrusts it into bag fears to look at a widow. This only shows that even a hunter shares the widespread superstitions in the society. He is not anything unlike other men. He hunts because he has to feed his family that way. Generally hunters of hares and birds, snake-catchers and snake charmers are from tribal families whose living conditions are extremely poor.

Let us observe the snake charmer. He is a skinny skeleton. He sits beneath the canopy of a tamarind tree. A canopy implies the uppermost layer of a forest forming a continuous layer of foliage. Seated beneath the canopy of the tree, is the skinny skeleton a god? Canopy is the cloth covering held on the head of a throne. Is that skinny skeleton a king with difference? The tamarind tree has many legends woven around it. Some say it is the daughter of the creator. Again some people think that it attracts ghosts. Thus the image of the skinny skeleton under the tamarind tree is loaded with ambiguity. It might be a sacred idol. Again it might be an uncanny figure. He is as it were a lone sentinel in a cluster of huts 'beneath a canopied tamarind tree'. If a skinny skeleton is the lone sentinel of the cluster of huts the readers can guess the economic plight of the denizens of the huts. The sentinel of the huts pours breath into a gourd pipe -

> which like a medieval magic wand
> spread its charm of music grand
> that embosomed thrill and threat;   (p.25)

The dispersed human habitation in a table land is aroused from its siesta by the gourd pipe that fills the landscape with thrill and threat. The alliteration of the fricative 'th' suggests the vibratory movement and the excitement spread far and wide. The poet here strikes a note that is at the same time thrilling and fearsome. Surely a terrible beauty is being born. There are no so-called entertainments in the dispersed habitations as we find in towns and cities. But they have the entertainments of their own. Woken up by the gourd pipe, the young and the old gather around the skinny skeleton below the canopy of the tamarind tree. Their gazes are directed to a bamboo basket beside the skinny skeleton. The skinny skeleton opens the lid of the basket. And lo!

> The cobra the vanquished captive
> Emerges like blind Samson
> Hissing in vain in vengeance
> Raising its dreaded hood
> With all its mortal fangs removed;   (p.25)

Yes the cobra the vanquished captive emerges like blind Samson. The image of blind Samson is appropriate in this context to the highest degree. The name of Samson is made very familiar by Milton whose poetic play *Samson Agonistes* has caught the attention of so many readers from the date of its publication in seventeenth century. Just as Samson's hair was cropped off, so are the fangs of the cobra removed. With the same rage of blinded Samson among the Philistines the cobra shows up and unfurls its hoods. But while Samson's hair developed, the fangs of the cobra have not been rejuvenated. Hence the cobra hisses in vain and helpless -

> it dances unawares in tune
> with the uncanny music;   (p.25)

Well the snake cannot hear the snake charmer. But it appears that the snake dances to the tune of the snake charmer. That is why the poet observes that the snake dances 'unawares' to the tune. This raises the question of appearance and reality.

The imagery of the snake charmer and dancing snake has imports on many levels. In the Indian context snake is feared. But at the same time we worship them. The snakes function as the belt of Lord Shiva. The snake is coiled energy or *kulakundalini* that is in every human body. Every snake that we espy without is but the externalization of the *kulakundalini* within. It is the coiled up primordial dormant energy in every human and with the practice of yoga it awakens as a furious hissing serpent and raises the awakened sleeping spiritual force (kundalini) from its slumber at the base of the spine up to the culminating point of the pineal gland on the top of the head. *Kulakundalini* stands for the individuality of every man. This individuality is being throttled everywhere. But its undying rage might pull down the mighty establishment raised by the self-seeking Philistines. True that for the time being the snake is helpless in the hands of the snake charmer. The dance of the snake might send us this dire message; the skinny skeleton of the snake charmer also makes some of us bow to him. Because is he not a minion of Lord Shiva.?

The poem ends in bathos. For all the risk he courts he gets a handful of rice. The perennial poverty of the tribal people like snake charmer is presented in its three-dimensional reality. While horror films earn millions, the snake charmer can hardly keep the wolf away from the doors. Fully knowing that catching the highly poisonous cobra is a dangerous adventure he volunteers and catches with professional skill and for all the risk he takes he gets only a handful of rice. He represents all such people whose hazardous work goes totally ignored. There are many other occupations where life is at risk. Are they well paid?

Chapter 3: Urban Phase

Having gone through in detail Dr. Reddy's portrayal of Indian rural life, now let us turn our attention to his presentation of the urban life. This comparative study is needed for a comprehensive understanding of the poetry of Reddy vis-à-vis that of others of the contemporary period. He sticks to the principle of truth in whatever he attempts to write and it is indeed a great virtue. There are many others who speak one thing and do the opposite and propagate values they never practice. Reddy is opposed to such theoretical pronouncements; what he believes he says and what he says he practices and that is the nature of T.V. Reddy whether in life or in his writings. Moreover he is a shrewd observer of men and matters and even trivial matters cannot escape from his gaze, which is indeed a great virtue of any good writer.

There are poems in this collection on hospitals and birthday functions. The flourishing of corporate hospitals is now a part of urban life and this corporate culture has entered into the fabric of metropolitan life; it has come to such a stage where the two cannot be separated from each other. In the same way celebrating birthday parties has become the fashion of the day in towns and cities and it is gradually spreading its influence in rural areas too. Urban life full of din and bustle presents a sharp contrast to the quiet atmosphere of the village life. Nowadays large numbers of people are seen migrating from villages to towns in search of some employment or some work in order to earn their livelihood. Urban life has its own advantages and attractions for the modern man on account of its wider sphere of activities and opportunities.

Then and Now

We have read women in different roles and they are not happy anywhere. A country's development does not consist of the wealth in the country's wallet or exchequer. Nor does it depend on the distribution of wealth among the masses. In short the development of a country does not depend on its GDP. The true development of a country is determined by the happiness index. Look at the landscape of the villages in India. The wells are dry. For a pot of water women have to walk long distances, sometimes a few kilometres and it is a regular feature in some of the remote villages in our country. The majestic peepal tree, the symbol of India's heritage and culture, that stands as the sentinel of a village has its branches dry. So the villages in India are defenceless. In Indian context villages are the backbone of India, but now these villages have become weak, feeble and helpless; in other words this backbone for all practical purposes appears to be broken and this is the irrevocable truth of this incredible India!

Economics derived from *oikonomos* means the management of hearth and home. Housewives or stay-at- home mothers are commonly in charge of home management. If after a whole day's drudgery they are destined to be drubbed by their drunken hubbies, if landlords look upon them with lust, if they seek to fill their starved stomachs with hopes without hope, if they cannot procure water for their family, if they cannot light the candle with the advent of evening, how could the country's wealth and happiness be on the rise? Unless the fortunes of women of the country are lifted up the economy of a country will ever remain lying on mud and blood at the ground zero level. But things were not like this in the past. Dr. Reddy throws light on this issue in his revealing poem 'Then and Now'. Earlier the attitude of men towards women was different:

> Then
> man strived,
> generated fire with stone
> to feed and shelter his woman;   (p. 31)

It was Morgan who introduced the three stages of history - savagery, barbarism and civilization. He divided and defined the stages by technological inventions. When man used fire, bow and pottery, he was savage. When man learnt agriculture and domestication of animal he was barbaric. When man learnt alphabet and writing he was civilized. Taking the cue from Morgan, should we say that now that man has computer literacy he is post-civilized? A mafia has a car whereas me a primary school teacher rides a cycle. Is the mafia more civilized than me a primary school teacher? In fact an illiterate person could be more civilized than a so-called civilized guy. True civilization depends on the culture of the heart. The primitive man belonging to the Paleolithic age and Neolithic age was more civilized than us because they cared for women, the home makers. Look at the modern woman. She follows her man to parties as a keyed skinny doll. She has no identity of her own, she has no individuality of her own. This is not all. While women strive to put on light in the hearth and make life at home exciting, men burn the women. Yes, this is both metaphorically and literally true.

Did we not find the new bride tossing between hopes and hopelessness, her heartbeats becoming fast. Her parents were weeping in a corner of the marriage hall when the hall was loud with pomp and pageantry. The parents had to borrow money to get their daughter married. But even after marriage the bridegroom's family might ask for more money from the bride. And as a consequence many newlywed women have to commit suicide often pouring kerosene oil on their bodies. Or else the bridegroom and his relatives burn her and commit culpable homicide. Such dowry deaths are not rare in India, Iran, Pakistan and Bangladesh. In 2010, 8399 such deaths were reported in India. In the words of Dr. Reddy women try to light their hearth while man burns his woman to feed his lust. The lust is not merely for the flesh but also for gold.

By the by Indian women rank third in the world for beating their husbands.1 Earlier man and woman belonged to each other. Their affirmed union brought tears of joy to their heart (cp. 'A Miracle', p.30). But now man and woman have been decoupled and in our modern society the number of divorces is increasing at an alarming rate. 'Divorce' which was unheard of in the previous generation has now become a common thing; Dr. Reddy exclaims -

> The new man of the plastic age!
> As their inner selves part
> she follows him to parties
> as a keyed skinny doll;   (p.31)

Dr. Reddy finds—

> A humble Eve
> treading the infernal steps
> of the resurrected Adam.   (p.31)

Earlier Eve violated the commands of God and partook of the fruit of knowledge. Adam partook of the fruit only at the instance of Eve so that he could also share with Eve the wrath of God. This was human and heroic. But now the resurrected Adam, thanks to civilization, leads her along the way to Inferno. Eve is simply following him. Thus there has been the reversal of role and it is the modern outlook, isn't it?

Birth Day Party

We are passing through a queer time. Now-a-days expenditure on overhead exceeds the expenditure on the production of a commodity. Rituals in religion stand for the overhead that is displayed. The main produce of spiritual quest has its cover up in religious rituals. With the Indians nowadays, ritual is more important than the spiritual import of the same. This we have experienced at the marriage party in the temple hall or marriage hall. The same experience could be gathered at the birthday party of a child. While the marriage party belongs to the middleclass, the birthday party of the child tells us of the hoopla created by the rich.

As per Hindu ritual the birth day should be the relevant day of the lunar month. It is on this day that the child should release living fishes to swim back to the river or the pond. The birds should be let loose from the cage. Plants should be watered. Fresh seeds should be sown. Alms should be distributed among the poor. Prayers should be addressed to the skies, to the stars especially to the constellation during the rise of which the child was born. But birthday parties are observed in India along just the opposite way, the product of the Western impact. In the olden days the celebration of a birth day was a rare feature and most of the people owing to predominant illiteracy were almost oblivious of the actual date of their birth.

And in many cases date of birth was not actually recorded by the parents and whatever date teacher wrote at the time of admission of the child in the school became the officially recorded date of birth. Dr. Reddy is fully aware of this naked truth and knows that this is what had happened in the case of his close friends and associates also. But nowadays with the sharp rise in literacy date of birth is recorded at the time of birth and its validity is unquestionable. In the modern times parents feel it is a matter of prestige to celebrate their child's birth day and they celebrate it according to their resources in varying degrees in a competitive way. In the light of the existing social scenario let us have a glimpse of the birthday party as seen through the poet Dr. Reddy.

There is the pandal, a bowing miniature sky. Man in his empty vaunt seeks the sky to bow over his head. Thunder only bursts from the skies. And here the thundering mike roars. The sky is studded with stars. And here the miniature sky is studded with mini-bulbs. Nature is outdone with human technology. Is it not mock heroic? When a wimp puts on the robes of Hector, is he not a buffoon? When man imitates the sky in the form of a pandal he is a buffoon. There is as it were daylight in the night. Nero fiddles when Rome burns. And the visitors at the party are rich. They have come to the party by cars. Their cars are parked on the road itself. If people find it difficult to go along the road, what would be the condition? Sophisticated shadows flock the hall. This reminds us of ladies, coming and going, talking of Michel Angelo in Eliot's poem 'Prufrock'. But the poet's focus is not on that aspect there. He simply sees the sophisticated men and women as it were on the glasses of aesthetic detachment just as the Lady of Shallot saw the world reflected on the mirror. They have come to celebrate the birthday of a bed-wetting child. And the poet finds the hands shake with hands. With that smiles expand; lips lisp while candles blink. The poet hears the glasses clang to the loud beauty of bangles of showcase dolls amid dance and caress. This shows that women have been robbed of their individuality.

> Lips lisped while candles blinked,
> glasses clang to the loud beauty
> of the bangles of show-case dolls;
> amid alien dance and caresses
> the east and the west debauched' (p.4)

The word 'debauched' is significant here. The culture that is revealed at the birthday party shows that it leads astray from both western values and native values. It is a bloodless imitation of the west. It is a travesty of values and culture.

Was not the party a birthday party to celebrate the birthday of the baby? While the lords and ladies danced apparently celebrating the birthday of the baby, the baby cried lustily on its damp bed. But no one paid any heed to it. This is why we said that in such celebrations the overhead expenditure was more and there was no real substance below the overhead. The cry of the baby has been buried beneath the thrown away leaves and tipsy looks. This only shows the ugly self of the rich society in India that has plunged in fun and feast. The whole celebration was a hollow sham. Towards its close everyone wished many happy returns of the day. These words were not merely static words, they are lifeless and stereotyped, parrot-like words. Do we the readers ever dream of such days where a crying baby is ignored amidst dance and songs of beaus and belles? We do not want that such days should return. The hollowness of the words—'many happy returns'—figures at the void created by the noisy celebration. The banquet hall with all its paraphernalia is weighed down with the lingering ashes of haunting status that sought to checkmate the cycle of time.

A party is generally a gathering of people to celebrate some event. A birthday party is held on the anniversary of a birthday. The present poem 'Birthday Party' opens with thundering mike. Lightning and thunder are indications of the might of Yahovah. God speaks through thunder. With some famous scripture thunder and lightning are angels. The thundering mike however apes the voice of God. The skies are the abode of God. And there is a bowing miniature sky bright with the flood of mini-bulbs. The phrase 'bowing sky' is significant. It speaks of bending or downward stooping sky in greeting, consent, courtesy, submission or veneration. Note that the thundering mike cannot cause the real sky to bend. The real sky is star-studded. Instead there is the artificial sky bowing. It is alight with mini bulbs. It reminds of the universe with heaven conjured for Trisanku. Let us see how well the artificial universe fares where heaven bends to greet the extraordinarily proud and ambitious man. The street on which the artificial universe is raised is blocked by a fleet of cars implying that every Tom, Dick and Harry do not have the right to enter into the artificial universe. Until and unless ye be rich and have cars ye cannot enter into this universe.

From harmony, heavenly harmony this universal frame began. In close imitation of the same the artificial universe made by man is drowned in gales of bizarre music. The music is however bizarre unlike the cosmic harmony. In this music-torn, microphone-loud artificial universe, aglitter with mini bulbs, everything real has been transformed into two dimensional entities. It is a transmogrifying vision. It reminds one of the lines of Robert Burns:

> See Social-life and Glee sit down,
> All joyous and unthinking,
> Till, quite transmogrified, they're grown
> Debauchery and Drinking.

In Reddy's poem we see—Hands shake, smiles expand and lips lisp while candles flash on and off in an intermittent way. These are all seen as phantoms in the blinking candle. Whispers are heard from lips lisping:

> 'Lips lisped while candles blinked,

> Glasses clank to the loud beauty
> of bangles of show case dolls;
> amidst dance and caresses
> the East and the West debauched;' (p.4)

Both are debauched, characterized by excessive indulgence in sex and alcohol. No one code of conduct is observed. Dr. Reddy thus creates an eerie atmosphere where ghosts and phantoms gambol. Ironically enough they are but real men and women of our everyday life transformed so. What makes them transformed into phantoms plunged in infernal glee? It is the birth day function of a bed-wetting child. In this loud and shadowy atmosphere the baby weeps lustily. But no one pays attention to it and the baby's cry becomes a cry in wilderness:

> The cry of the baby on the damp bed
> Got buried beneath the dunghill
> Of thrown away leaves and tipsy looks;   (p.4)

The cry of the baby likens the refuse like thrown away leaves of plates in which food was served amid tipsy looks. Is this how we welcome a baby? Is this how we should welcome the child Jesus or the child Krishna? With us rituals are hollow sham. Their real meaning is lost. We take the rituals as opportunities to gratify our own senses. Think of the ghosts dancing when a human baby is born. This is singularly ominous for the new born babe. Gradually the orgy comes to its omega. The banquet hall is deserted. The pious wish—'Many happy returns of the day'—reverberates in silence. In other words many such birthdays of the child should take place and every year they will doff their human robes to play their elemental roles of phantoms. In other words this is a horrid society where we breathe. It is keen to destroy every creative force of every baby by way of using its birth to celebrate the feast of Hecate. Modern civilization is the priest of Hecate in the disguise of a pious devotee of human values. Birth day is no more than a convenient pretext to exhibit one's itch for the display of one's wealth and sphere of influence and their social circle.

The Hospital

Dr. Reddy is a harsh critic of different institutions prevalent in India. He has dwelled on the dire situation of the rural working women. In the farm she works hard in the scorching Sun. The land lord has eyes on her youth. Her heart on the other hand is engrossed with the child whom she has left in the hut. Back home she shall undergo a beating from her drunken husband. Dr. Reddy has exposed the ugliness of the dowry system. Temples as an institution function only to support the system. It does not support the poor. Such entertainments as birthday parties only lay bare the ugliness of the so-called civilized society of the rich. In the selfsame way he has uncovered the truth below the surface of the therapeutic system of the country in his revealing poem 'The Hospital'.

The poem is a dramatic lyric written in mock-heroic style. It opens in the media res. A patient is lying on a hospital bed. In other words there has been a patient in the hospital bed for days together. Surely he is ailing. But despite his stay at the hospital for days together his condition has not improved an iota. In India medical treatment is costly. Lot of money is spent for getting a bed and for being nursed and doctored. The expenditure on medicines is also enormous. Be that as it may, despite lot of expenditure on up-keeping a patient the patient may not show any improvement as to his complaints. In the present case it has been a 'senseless stay' for the patient. There is a pun in the word senseless. The patient may have had no sense for a fortnight. Or else his stay at the hospital for a fortnight has been bootless or meaningless since he has not improved even a grain.

In this crucial situation, crucial for the patient who has been senseless for a fortnight, the chief doctor shows up:

> The chief doctor burning a cigar
> With decades of decadent experience
> Gives his Delphic oracle   (p.3)

Mark the overbearing antics of the chief doctor. He has decades of decadent experience. It provokes laughter in the reader. How come that a doctor becomes the chief doctor if he has decades of decadent experience? In India it is possible. The higher you go up in hierarchy you are removed from field work. Sermon from the Areopagus is all that you can deliver if you are promoted to the higher rung of the hierarchy. Hence your experience becomes decadent. And when with decadent experience you deliver the prognosis of a disease imitating the Delphic oracle, is it not mock-heroic? When trifles are decked in sublime cover it is mock-heroic.

The readers are curious to know what the oracle says. Well the patient is shifted to the ICU or intensive care unit of the hospital. In the context of Indian readers the very suggestion of intensive care unit sends a cold wave through the veins, because ICU is very costly for even the upper middle class people. Now what happens after the patient is shifted to ICU??

> All tests are conducted
> Diagnosis seems to reach its destination
> Treatment continues round the clock
> For the probable disease (p.3)

Unless the patient is shifted to the intensive care all tests are not conducted. This is funny. When bureaucratic rules are observed in a hospital, the hospital has no human face.

> Some nurses treat like real sisters
> While their seniors in white robes
> Behave like white elephants (p.3)

Well when all the tests are performed treatment continues round the clock on the basis of probable disease. Fine; diagnosis seems to reach its own destination. What does that mean?

> Nine-tenths of their knowledge
> Assumes it to be a type of tetanus
> While the remainder suggests meningitis
> Still a fraction roams in ambiguity
> A larger cloudy canvas, the nebula; (p.3)

Here Dr. Reddy throws a floodlight on the notion of causality in medical science and diagnosis of disease. The doctor does not listen to what the patient says non-verbally and what he wants to say verbally. Statistics cannot lead us far. A fraction of ambiguity is enough to disrupt the whole effort of treating a disease which is essentially ambiguous but hypothetically diagnosed. Medical science fails to face the uncertainty element in the procedure of diagnosing illness. In practice medical science seldom avails itself of intuition. But in fact gut feelings and qualitative research could be of great help to sincere doctors. Be that as it may, the fraction of the uncertainty makes the narrative full of suspense. The priest prays at bedside.

> On the road of trial and error
> One quizzical drug cures the patient
> and drowns the profession in wonder. (p.3)

But the doctors quickly recover from their amazement and pride themselves while the disease moves elsewhere. Someone else contracts the disease. There is a pun in the use of the word contract. Contract means agreement. And indeed every disease is psychosomatic. The poet has personified disease. Disease is a force that overwhelms the living body. Does he thereby mean that a force parallel to the disease-force needs to be charged into the diseased body to drive away the disease? Thus the poem not only opens to the view the state of therapeutic system in India, but also raises pertinent questions regarding the philosophy behind medical science.

Now let us discuss the poem from another angle. There are heroic poems hailing the conquest of countries by kings and princes. *Raghuvamsam* is a Sanskrit epic that dwells on the conquests of Raghu who belonged to solar dynasty. There are heroic poems that delineate the defence of a country against the invaders. The Vikings invaded England. The Anglo Saxons despite displaying great prowess could not hold out against the invaders. Here is a story of invasion which failed. The story has been narrated from the perspective of the victim of aggression. But who is the aggressor here? It is neither Sohrab, nor Rustum, nor Alexander, nor the Vikings. It is a disease that is the aggressor.

The invasion of a disease is more terrible than the attack by a human conqueror. Think of Marlowe's Tamburlaine. He conquers Persia and Turkey. He defeats the sultan of Egypt and the king of Arabia. He destroys Babylon. But finally Tamburlaine is struck by illness and dies. So disease at some point remains unconquerable and is famed to conquer world conquerors who are destined simply to lick the dust. A disease does not ordinarily attack a country unless it is an epidemic. The human body is the object of conquest in the dreams of a disease. Here in this poem a body is besieged by a disease. A living body besieged by a disease is known as a patient. The place where the battle between the besieging diseases and the living body and its friends, the doctors and nurses, takes place is a hospital.

The poem 'Hospital' opens in media res and presents before us the patient and the patient's present condition in simple and unadorned words. The poet without resorting to any devious or descriptive language presents the situation directly and the beauty lies in its simplicity as the context demands simple diction:

> The case remains the same
> No change in the patient's condition   (p.3)

That is, a besieged living body has been long in the battlefield called hospital. Just as Homer did not dwell on the siege of Troy from its outset so our poet does not dwell on the battle at the hospital in response to the siege of the living body from its very beginning.

> The chief doctor burning a cigar
> With his decades of decadent experience
> Gives his Delphic oracle
> After a fortnight's senseless stay (p.3)

In other words the besieged living body has been lying in the battlefield known as hospital senseless for last fifteen days; or else, it made no sense for the living body under siege to remain in the hospital for fifteen days. The pun in the use of the word 'senseless' creates a humorous effect even when a person is seriously ill, senseless and bedridden. The future of the patient is uncertain. At this crucial juncture between life and death the Delphic oracle is consulted. Delphi is an ancient city of ancient Greece. So the hospital we guess is a grand old building on which senility is writ large signified by fissures and cracks. It might remind one of a temple of Apollo bent with antiquity. The hospital is thus both a battlefield and a place where an oracle is consulted. In the temple of Apollo; the high priestess of Apollo also serves as an oracle.

The battlefield is a place where if one dies embraces heaven and if one wins one enjoys the world. Here in the battlefield the chief of the defenders of the living body is the chief doctor. And he serves as the oracle. He burns a cigar with decades of decadent experience. Pythia, the high priestess of Apollo, was famed to have taken fumes from the crevices of a rock. Hidden behind the crevices was the corpse of a python that was killed by Apollo. The fumes of the cigar are charged with decades of decadent experience. Does the imagery speak of the fumes of the dead serpent rotting for long ages? The chief doctor must have experienced the decay and destruction of many a body through decades. A venerable old man indeed! Consequently in the ICU of the emergency ward all tests are conducted.

This elaborate ritual conducted reminds one of the elaborate rituals observed by the high priestess of Delphi such as washing in the nearby Castalian spring, burning laurel leaves and drinking holy water. These rituals would take a whole day for the priestess. And we can cogently imagine that the various tests to help the patient were conducted for a long time, leaving us the onlookers anxiously torn with expectations. The diagnosis seems to reach its destination. Destination is the place where one should visit or where one is expected to visit. Diagnosis seems to reach its destination or failure to diagnose.

Delphic oracle used to speak in ambiguous terms and speak in a trance. Authors who mentioned this oracle were Aeschylus, Aristotle, Clement of Alexandria, Diogenes, Diodorus, Euripides, Herodotus, Julian Justin, Sophocles, Plato, Lucan, Ovid and others. To these great names another name is being added. That is, Reddy's. With Reddy Delphic oracle was as it were the pronouncements of the chief doctor of a hospital.

> Treatment continues round the clock
> Nine tenths of their knowledge
> Assumes it to be a type of tetanus
> While the remainder suggests meningitis
> Still a fraction roams in ambiguity.   (p.3)

If the state of a patient is determined as a case of tetanus and again as a case of meningitis, how could the treatment of the patient take place? Naturally the heads of doctors and the friends of the patient roam in ambiguity. In other words their heads reel in a larger cloudy canvas, the nebula. The nebula could mean in two ways—1. a cloud of gas and dust which is bright but indistinct or which is dark silhouette against luminous objects; 2. a clouded spot in the cornea causing defective vision. In other words the failure to diagnose might be due to the fact that the disease cannot be distinctly analyzed or else due to the fact that the doctors suffer from defective eyesight. Be that as it may, treatment continues round the clock. Is it not foolish to treat a patient without knowing from what disease he suffers? The high profile doctors are thus no better than hacks. Now the disease is being fought heroically by a handful of hacks or by a handful of white collar people in the robes of knight-at-arms deeming themselves as the greatest heroes in the world. A comic sight! In addition to Pythia there were other personnel at the temple of Delphi. And here too there are senior and junior nurses to look after the patient and assist the doctor:

> Some nurses treat like real sisters
> While their seniors in white robes
> Behave like white elephants, ...   (p.3)

In other words these senior nurses are of no use, but they are highly paid or in other words expensive. And there are fresh doctors who are like the new hatched chicks in the plumage of the young Chanticleers or cocks of fairy tales. They are like crows in peacock's plumes. They take airs winking at their studious stethoscopes or breasts. In other words they are braggarts with inflated breasts. So while these Don Quixotes and Sancho Panzas are charging the disease without knowing whether it is a windmill or an ogre, the priest prays to the Great Healer for recovery of the patient. May be, the priest too is not serious about his job. May be he is the same priest who presided over the wedding in the poem 'The Indian Bride' and saw borrowed money in the flames. Thus to put it in simple words, a set of half-learned fools in the borrowed robes of the wise venture to cure a mysterious disease. It is like fighting a machine gun with a sword. And the death of the victim lies in the logic of affairs. We readers are impelled to pray to God for the rescue of the patient. And lo! Peripeteia, a regular aspect of Greek tragedy marking a turning point, takes place. The patient is recalled to life!

> On the road of trial and error
> one quizzical drug cures the patient
> and drowns the profession in wonder;   (p.3)

But they are not late for taking the credit for rescuing a patient from the attack of an incurable disease. Though the patient's recovery is beyond the limited knowledge of the doctors, probably against their situational expectation, they are quick to take the credit of the patient's recovery.

In ancient time Delphic oracle was at the centre of the society. Now people do not believe in oracles. They go to hospitals for the prognosis of their disease and cure. So hospitals are at the centre of the society. Reddy describes the Delphic oracle in terms of modern hospitals and modern hospitals in terms of Delphic oracle. This is a great literary feat and figurative triumph in the realm of poetic art. The whole poem has been hewn in the pattern of mock-heroic poetry. But what happens to the disease? Disease is a character here. It reminds us of Morality plays of Middle English literature. Nothing can annihilate evil and disease. The vanquished victor proudly marches in search of a fresh contract. The pun in the word contract is obvious. One contracts a disease. Could it also mean that until and unless a patient subconsciously welcomes a disease there can be no disease.

The Thanatos of a man often subconsciously wishes that he should have a disease. Besides, is the disease in search of a fresh contract between the Death's minion Mephistopheles and itself? Finally is not the world a vanity fair of which the self-conceited doctors and nurses and the hospitals are incarnations? Self conceit and ignorance are the bane that vitiates the way of the world. One common feature of our Hospitals in India is the lack of professional ethics. Vast majority of doctors of medical profession are money-minting machines and their only objective is acquisition of money through all possible ways. Moral responsibility is thrown at four winds. In the West if something goes wrong in the treatment the doctor is sued and action is taken; in India even if many patients die in the hands of a doctor on account of his sheer negligence or ignorance there is no one to ask him and he goes scot-free under the defensive cover of Karma theory. No wonder in the statement of George Bernard Shaw, one of the greatest intellects of twentieth century: 'Doctors are licensed murderers!' (vide his play *Doctor's Dilemma*).

Let the Eyes Be Shut

> Let my eyelids /Close or seal themselves/
> In intensive intercourse /Or mute mutiny /
> against alien invasion /or distracting digital dust/
> from the traffic-jammed roads /of drunken dragons/
> let the eyes be shut /lest they should be distracted/
> from pleasant illusions /by elusive eerie delusions.   (p.6)

While people want to remain wide awake and have their eyes wide open to register the world as it is laden with beauty and ugliness, the poet wishes that his eyes be shut in intensive intercourse which indeed is essentially of philosophical nature. The word 'intercourse' is a double-edged sword. To a mind at the gross level intensive intercourse means slow intercourse or slow sex. At a deeper level intercourse implies communication with the other till for a time the distinction between the self and the non-self is erased. The difference is wiped off under the impact of an ecstasy which is spiritual in essence. And during this intense intercourse one had better shut his or her eyes imbued in a sense of security that is seldom found in the humdrum of life.

The poet wants his eyelids sealed so that the communion is not interrupted by any jarring sight or a sight that represents an entirely worldly subject or object generating carnal or material interest. Shutting the eyes implies a mute mutiny against alien invasion or distracting dust from the traffic-jammed roads of distracting dragons and all types of distractions arising from the indiscriminate usage of the digital system and technology. The self is a denizen of a world ruled by the hurly-burly of existence where traffic-jammed roads of dragons throw dust in the eyes and blind them or mislead them. Traffic jams clearly stand for obstacles on the way of the pilgrim. The self openly but silently defies this hurly-burly of worldly life, this materialistic life that leads to the shutting of one's eyes to the power of discrimination and to the brighter aspects of higher life.

In fact the human body or the bone-house is a castle with nine gates in which the self is sheltered. The poet imagines that the body is under siege by the sights and sounds of the world without. The poet shuts the gates of his bone house. The eyes are the two of those gates. Now free from any interruption from the world without the poet can plunge into the slow intercourse with the other or the world within. Nay, so far it seemed that the poet shuts out the world without to plunge into slow or intensive intercourse with the other and there would be a yin-yang, but not so. There is the peripeteia or sudden reversal of our expectations. No higher planes are reached by shutting the world out. The poet prefers delusions despite being contradicted by reality. And surely they are difficult to realize. They are elusive. May be, he sees women with pitchers brimming with water, new brides bright with happiness, hospitals loud with cheers of the patients recalled to life and vivacity. When the eyes are shut the inward eye opens.

May be the poet sees these vignettes with his inward eye. But they are elusive delusions. Be that as it may, the poet shuts out the traffic-jammed roads that obstruct the poet on his way to inner reform. And he is plunged in the world of make-believe and he does not want to be distracted from his reverie. He knows the present world is fully infested with the craze for the digital communication and clearly the world now has become a digital world. This the poet as a seer had foreseen as early as in the year of composition of the poetical work and he wants to keep himself away from the distractions of digital world and from the infection of the 'digital dust'- a symbolical expression yielding layers of meaning.

Thus the poem is ruthlessly realistic. It has seen with its baleful eyes the horrors of the waking world. It seeks to take refuge in reverie. But in the dream itself the poem is aware of the fact that the visions he espies are but elusive. Hence there is no escape from the harsh realities of existence in work-a-day-world or in dreams. The poem at a deeper level reminds us of the profoundly significant lines of *Bhagavad Gita* which mean what appears to be dark for the worldly people is light for the sage and what appears to be light yielding sensual pleasures for ordinary beings is indeed the result of ignorance for the sage:

>Ya Nisa sarva bhutanam tasyam jagarti samyami
>Yasyam jagriti bhutani sa nisa pasyato munehi. (2-69)

It can be translated as -

>What is night for all the living beings is the wakeful state for the *muni*
>Wakeful state of the beings is the night for the *muni* or sage'.

Chapter 4: Political and Social Phase

Poems of T.V. Reddy are a veritable treasure house of his critical perception of the various aspects of political and social life in the country. Being a responsible citizen he could not be blind to the contemporary situation whether it is political or social, cultural or religious, economic or educational. His active participation in all the activities becomes clear as we go through his poems and no part of life can escape from his critical observation; he does not spare either the schemes of the Government and activities of political leaders irrespective of their party affiliations or the attitude of the citizens, both the rich and the poor alike. The excess of greed of the political leaders and their unscrupulous ways in acquiring and hoarding heaps and heaps of ill-gotten wealth is exposed by the poet at every stage. He does not exempt even teaching profession to which he belongs and which he served with dedication for above four decades.

His satirical attack on the commercial nature of most of the privately managed schools and technical and management colleges is realistic to the core and vehemently criticizes corporate culture which is based on exploitation. The corruption of the bureaucrats and employees in general is exposed at every stage in bold strokes. He says the true spirit of democracy has disappeared from the boundaries of this country since elections have become more or less a farce with the active role of money and liquor in purchasing voters and their votes. What is quite remarkable and commendable in T.V. Reddy is the fact that his satire at these self-seeking political leaders and at the selfish public is drawn with courage and conviction and his satirical ability compels comparison with the famous Augustan satirists Dryden and Pope. Among Indian poets in English there is no other poet who makes use of the weapon of satire as deftly as Dr. Reddy employs and it is here that he excels others.

'In Exile' & 'Democratic Lines'

Hunting is an occupation like fishing. The fisherman with his angler catches fish in sea and river while the hunter kills fowl and hare in the woods and air. That is how we can distinguish a hunter from a fisherman. On the surface their occupations are cruel no doubt. But they pursue such occupations for their livelihood. Hunter is a hunter and fisherman is a fisherman. You know them by their appearance. They do not hide their identity. But think of a politician. He is a professional dissembler shining in borrowed robes. The fisherman offers food as bait for the fish. Once the fish is drawn to it the fish is trapped and killed. The politicians do not catch fishes. They catch votes from the masses. Though they revel in this cruel profession, apparently they do not appear to revel in any cruel occupation as they take shelter in democracy which lends an impression of dignity though it is now divorced from the essential virtue of decency.

From the hide out of democracy the politician throws the bait of spurious currency notes with lolling tongues. How do you know a politician? He has a stretched tongue. He is puffed by longing lungs and rolling cans of liquors. While the fisherman and the hunter kill or ensnare fish and birds for their livelihood politicians trap the fisherman and the innocent hunter with the decoy of spurious currency and liquor; thereby they ensnare and enslave human values. They dangle the bait of spurious currency and compel poor men to give up human values for material gains. Entrapping fish is to kill them. Entrapping men is to rob them of their human values. And this is not all. They sell the souls of the common men to Lust and Mammon. They auction the souls of the masses at the floor of the depraved Assembly.

In other words the politicians sell the hopes and emotions of a common man which are sacred and private to him to the highest bidder at a public place, in front of a depraved or corrupt assembly. The assembly could mean legislature where the politicians assemble to decide the fate of the masses. And the depraved assembly could allude to Augustine of Hippo. In fact the assembly of powerbrokers are those men after the Fall of Man who cannot but choose to sin.

Milton gives us vivid portraits of the fallen angels who assembled in the pandemonium. The political leaders are but their minions. They sell the souls of their fellowmen to Mephistopheles. They are fleshy and they trade in flesh. Imagine an assembly of fleshy guys with stretched tongues trading in flesh and rolling in smuggled fleshly comforts! In this big bazaar of flesh trade -

> As integrity becomes crippled
> hypocrisy climbs atop the ladder
> and reigns supreme in seers garb
> mocking at honesty in exile.   (In Exile, p. 28)

In the present day world the virtue of integrity or the quality of being honest is virtually on the wane. Strong moral principles vanish. No wonder, in such material conditions and circumstances dishonesty flourishes. Hypocrisy in the robes of a seer rules the world. They simply lampoon and ridicule honesty. Is there any honest man? If any, he is in exile. This is a morality drama where abstract ideas are protagonists.

Thus the poem dwells on the occupation of the common man such as a hunter or a fisherman. Next it dwells on the rulers of these common rung of men. While others live on the flesh of fish and birds and animals, these ruling class people i.e. the politicians live on the flesh of common men. Reddy highlights politics as a profession and lays bare its operation in the name of democracy. Under the spell of democracy the world has been bereft of good men. Good man, if any, is in exile. The title of the poem 'Exile' reminds us of the exile of Rama and of the Pandavas. Ours is really a wasteland, not because crops do not grow here, but because good men do not flourish here. They are banished from our world busy in acquiring by all means, hoarding and spending.

In the poem entitled 'In Exile' the poet tries to dissect the conduct of the present-day politicians as well as the existing system of democracy. He observes -

> But our professed leaders
> Professional dissemblers
> That shine in borrowed robes
> In the guise of democracy
> Catch peoples' unlettered votes
> With spurious currency notes   (p.28)

Democracy could be of two types—direct democracy and indirect democracy. In ordinary parole we mean indirect democracy by the word democracy. Democracy is that kind of political system where people elect their representatives from themselves only. The representatives of the people rule the people. How does the election take place? There could be many men who would like to rule the people. It is the people who will choose their representative among the many aspirants through the exercise of their right to vote—a formal indication of a choice. And the chosen representative becomes the part of the government.

Hence in order to be in the Government and in order to be an elected representative of the people one must catch votes from the people the way the fishermen catch fish or the hunters catch birds. How do they catch votes? They catch votes with spurious currency notes. What is spurious? Well anything that lacks authenticity. Therefore spurious currency notes are currency notes that are not disclosed to the government. So they catch votes in exchange of black money. Once they catch votes or assent of the people with black money the honesty and the human values of the people are suspended. They are sent to exile. Unless one has black money one cannot spend money to buy votes. Who has black money? One who aspires to be the people's representative amasses black money. The lines of the poem 'Democracy' throws more light on this aspect:

> He is masses' matinee idol
> the black marketeer and the banker
> the racketeer or the gambler
> an unruly student to whom
> academic books are untouchables
> or the cine actor rolling in black money
> to whom sacrifice is a strange word-   (p.33)

Generally poetic speech is used to exaggerate the intended idea or the implicit thought, but here there is no exaggeration. Mark what the Newsweek says:

The 14th Lok Sabha was the first in which it was crystal clear just how many members were alleged crooks. Thanks to new rules pushed into law by a group of fed-up college professors after years of resistance from dozens of political parties, candidates for the Lok Sabha for the first time had to disclose their assets and criminal records. The disclosures seemed to have little impact on the 2004 election: 128 of the 543 winners had faced criminal charges, including 84 cases of murder, 17 cases of robbery and 28 cases of theft and extortion. Many face multiple criminal counts—including one M.P. who faces 17 separate murder charges—and no major party is beyond reproach. This requirement of disclosure of one's assets is a new trend, but many members are not disclosing all their assets. Unless there is a fool-proof mechanism the truth will not come out. Most experts say the situation is deteriorating. "The general opinion is that the influence of criminals in politics is steadily increasing," says Himanshu Jha of the National Social Watch Coalition[1].

> He knows the trick of whipping passions
> Which he can trade to his greedy ends
> And encash the glamour to his success
> ...
> While masses groan under his vain promises
> His relatives revel in ill-gotten wealth;   (p.33)

The candidate who wants to represent the people must know the art of whipping up passions. He must be a demagogue par excellence loading his speeches with lies and he must know how to feather his own nest with the passions roused in the masses. And once he is elected how does he fare? He does not remember what he told the people to get elected by them. The prices of essential commodities might rocket up. The plight of the people in the face of price rise might be precarious. But he does not pay any heed to that. His regular diet consists of the most costly fruits and food. While the masses groan from hunger, his relatives rich in ill-gotten wealth revel in laughter. If he gets the opportunity to represent the people for one term only he makes money enough for future generations to live on.

Dr. Reddy uses heroic couplet reminiscent of Alexander Pope with great power and force to describe the real situation of the representative of men in the democratic system; in this aspect it is not an exaggeration to say that there is hardly a poet of Reddy's stature and ability in Indian English who can employ the device of satire to create the required effect of satire.

> Exhorting men to sacrifice gold and cash
> He liberally parts with a pinch of dusty ash.   (p.33)

This is an instance of bathos bathed in the facts of the real workings of democracy. May be, the term over, one representative is replaced by another. The latter also functions in the selfsame manner as his predecessor did. There is no room for the honest and altruistic souls to survive in the democratic system. Reddy's *In Exile* and *Democratic lines* are companion poems. Perhaps like Kent, Reddy could address democracy thus:

---

[1] www.newsweek.com/new-rules- expose-criminals-indias

> Fare thee well king, since thus thou wilt appear
> Freedom lives hence and banishment is here.

The poems 'Democratic Lines' and 'In Exile' reveal a very significant point. It goes without saying that unless there is democracy capitalism cannot thrive. The mode of the economic activities of a country depends on the political frame of that country. At the same time capitalism in its own interest invokes democracy. That is, the mode of economic activities in a country brings a political system in its trail. But Dr. Reddy's poems see into the truth of such notions. Capitalism in a word implies market and buying and selling. And when votes are bought and sold instead of commodities in a democratic system democracy chokes capitalism. Capitalism is not merely focused on the aspect of moneymaking by way of adding utility to the raw material things. Man is impelled by greed for power as well. Hence capitalism in trying to have power over the state machinery will be drawn to buying and selling votes and the buying and selling commodities for general use of the public will take backseat. Thus capitalism chokes democracy. This is never observed before in prose or rhyme, not even in economics or political system.

Dr. Reddy further points out the irony inherent in democracy. Are not the people buying votes with spurious money also criminals? If such men fill the legislature how can we expect the legislature to enact laws to instil discipline among the masses? In order that we make a state economically prosperous and democratically efficient there must be the rule of law.

Perhaps in order to learn what to buy and what to sell there should be the teachers. Economic activities of buying and selling cannot be left to the wants of the people. The people should be taught what they should want and what they should buy and sell. To that end moral education is a must for the producers and consumers. Hence the poet dwells on teaching profession.

The Teacher

If the politicians can lead the masses astray the teachers could check it. A teacher is like a candle. He transmits light to dark cavities. A teacher is nobler than a painter and a sculptor. Because a painting or a sculpture even at its best is deaf and dumb. But a teacher breathes life into living logs and moulds the erring minds into worthy beings of the species. He is an alchemist and he transforms base metals into precious ones with the alchemy of his words. The poet calls the teacher a magician, Words are his magic wand. True that the God Almighty created man and Nature. But to be a man biologically is not enough. It is merely a living log. To become a man in the right sense of the term every member of the homo-sapiens must have a teacher. A teacher completes the task of God by way of grooming the head and heart of every man.

One is apt to ask why despite such teachers is the world too much with us buying votes and selling votes? The answer is simple. Dr. Reddy has already pointed out that the state of affairs in the political and economic sphere has sent honesty and honest people to exile. The poem 'The Teacher' observes that the teacher is no longer in his element as he has to sing to the tunes of the Government who frame the syllabus. Virtually he has retired from the stage of social activity. Economics is a social science and the teacher can no longer exert his influence on the economy and politics of the society.

The poem 'The Teacher' is significant on another plane. It is autobiographical at the core. Dr. Reddy himself worked as a teacher for more than four decades and his father was also a dedicated teacher. The poem dwells on how he really felt like on the day of his retirement. It seemed that the mind of the teacher in him that struggled to emit light amidst the encircling gloom was made inane with the retirement. The classrooms that were loud with the musical voice of the teacher Dr. Reddy would no longer vibrate with it. Dr. Reddy knew that no one can remain in the chair for ever. Despite that when he had to retire he wished that time should stop. That is human; we men know that everything is subject to decay and death. Yet when our loved ones die we wish that time should have had stopped before the death. And this is not all. Often we wish that time should be retrograde. Dr. Reddy on his day of retirement might have wished that if possible he would retrace his steps back. Not that he wanted the employment to continue, but he would be deprived of the opportunity of the noble work of teaching and enlightening the student community and educating them in the right direction. But it is a pity that the good teachers have retired. Good men and great teachers are in a state of exile.

Noble is the role of a teacher and it finds a shining expression in Reddy's poem; forgetting all his personal problems, teacher with full dedication to the noble profession makes an earnest attempt to impart knowledge to his disciples:

> He transforms baser metal and ennobles

> With the alchemic power of his word
> Gift of the gab is his magic wand
> that does miracles and brings metamorphosis; (The Teacher, p.24)

Words are the tool for the teacher to transform men for a better world. In this democratic set up words have other uses and the poet has already shown how the present day political leaders misuse and abuse words for reaping a bumper harvest at the time of elections:

> In this set up of apparent democracy
> A multi-purpose word of lip service
> A baneful breath and abscess
> The greater the degree of hypocrisy
> The stronger the asset to be a leader
> (Democratic Lines, p.33)

Teacher's role is a nobler one and the role of an ideal teacher shines with divinity. While God creates the child it is the teacher who re-creates the child by filling child's mind with noble character and culture by imparting right education. That is why Hindu scriptures have given a higher pedestal to teacher and placed him next to mother and father and only next to teacher comes God. Sanatana Dharma considers teacher as a God—'Acharya Devobhavah!':

> If the Almighty creates, he re-creates
> and transforms the raw substance
> into a refined one, rich and noble;
> Through ages he is like a candle
> that burns and spreads light
> ignored and forgotten after its exit.

Right from the ancient days of Vedic period teacher or guru is accorded highest respect. Let us have a look at the ancient slokas:

> Guru Brahma Gurur Vishnuh/ Guru Devo Maheswarah/
> Guru Saakshaat Parabrahma/Tasmai Sri Gurave Namah//
> Agjnaana timirandhasya vyaaptam/ Gjnaana anjana salaakayaa/
> Chakshuhu unmiilatam yenam / Tasmai Sri Gurave Namah//

It can be translated into English in the following words:

> Guru is verily the representative of Brahma, Vishnu and Siva.
> He creates, sustains knowledge and destroys the weeds of ignorance.

> I salute such a guru.'
> A guru can save us from the pangs of ignorance (darkness)
> by applying to us the balm of knowledge or awareness of the Supreme.
> I salute such a guru.'

Such is the importance given to teacher or guru and teacher is expected to protect and preserve the splendour of the nobility of teaching profession; otherwise he cannot be a teacher in the true sense. If he fails in his role he is not worthy of the profession. It would be appropriate to remember the words of Albert Einstein on the role of teachers: "It is the supreme art of the teacher to awaken joy in creative expression and knowledge." In this context how can we forget the words of the great poet Wordsworth on the role of a teacher? In one of his letters he expressed—"Every great poet is a teacher; I wish either to be considered as a teacher or as nothing". Dr. Reddy speaks of the ideal teacher the meaning of which he fulfilled throughout his long career as a teacher. He really deserves the Best Teacher Award which he received from the Government of Andhra Pradesh which recognized his extraordinary merit as a dedicated teacher at the College and University level. Good teachers are never forgotten by his students and they remember him till the end. Next to the parents, it is the teacher alone who feels proud of his student when the student reaches a high position and acquires fame.

My Bare Needs

Indeed just as we use words to express ourselves, similarly can we use words to hide ourselves? And in fact if we had no words, if mankind had no words, we would not be the hypocrites we are. And in the absence of the teacher who uses words to transform baser metal of men into nobler one, the words of the politicians rule the world. They make vain promises. They promise to serve us the basic needs such as food, clothing and shelter. But these promises have been proved to be false through the decades of democracy in India. And hence the common man has been fed up with the lectures of the politicians—the vote mongers. Dr. Reddy speaks in the parole of the common man:

> Enough, enough,
> I want nothing
> I ask nothing   (My Bare Needs, p.26)

The plight of the common man is presented here in realistic colours. The existing situation in the country is portrayed here without any hyperbolic use of language. The poet comes down to the earthy level and presents the abject condition of the poor who are constantly deceived by the politicians of all parties with their systematized game of false propaganda and a barrage of lies. The politicians have filled the hungry bellies with pots of words which are lies. They have hijacked the thirsting hearts with vain promises. The starved men say that they are no longer hungry.

> My hunger migrated
> to the white fields
> while my bare needs
> get blasted by iconoclasts   (p.26)

White field is a Biblical imagery. It implies fields ready for harvest. Does the poet mean thereby that this hunger of the masses is ready for sowing the seeds of social and political revolution? One asks: Does not starvation draw tears in their eyes? No hope. The pot-bellied politicians flash upon their eyes all the time. The sight of the pot-bellies drives away their hunger and makes the poor forget their hunger temporarily. Their eyes are filled with the massive figures of the corpulent bodies of these leaders. When the leaders are not satisfied with all the food and wealth how can they think of the poor and hungry masses? The portrait of the politicians is recurrent in the poems. It becomes vivid in the reader's mind the way the portraits forged by Dryden come alive to the readers. That is why Reddy's satirical portraits are as fresh and lively as those of Dryden.

That Dr. Reddy is an excellent sculptor of words can be seen in the use of the symbolic word 'iconoclast'. Can there be any other word more appropriate and contextually meaningful and creative than this intuitively chosen word? This is the last straw that breaks poor man's back when his essential needs are blasted by these elected leaders who act as iconoclasts blasting the sacred images of the various roles of democracy visualized and revered by ordinary masses. When the leaders are always hungry of power and wealth how can they think of the basic hunger of the poor people? In other words the common man with basic needs unfulfilled is totally disillusioned with the leaders as well as the present system of democracy.

Shelter is one of the bare needs of the hungering masses. But the poet finds their huts blasted by cyclone. When dense drops from above ceaselessly continue they prepare a makeshift hollow hut to protect themselves from the freaks of Nature. But they can hear the rains. Breathless they hear the melting marching tune. Who else can come in battle array like a merciless Tamburlaine? In other words it seems apparently that the skies are colonized by the devils. Or else drops of manna are supposed to fall from the skies to rejuvenate man. Indeed so foul a weather we have not witnessed before. This very earth which is our hut is already blasted by cyclonic storm of pollution, radiation and want of compassion. The hut could stand for the bone house where the soul takes shelter. It has been shattered by the blasts of desire flung from the skies where Mammon and supermarkets rule.

A Form of Dirge

The poem 'A Form of Dirge' reminds us of the dirge of the dying year. The entire poem is skilfully woven around the beautiful image of the cyclone and the timing of the occurrence of the downpour of rain. Well, dirge in Shelley refers to the West Wind. The West Wind in Shelley brings about destruction. But with Shelley destruction is the precursor of fresh creation. Shelley wanted to be a leaf, a cloud or a wave to pant beneath the powers of the wild west wind. Here Dr. Reddy is sheltered in a hut at the zero hour when cyclone is to burst. The zero hour is the hour when a military operation is set to begin. The cyclone is a military operation as it were. The music of the downpour of rain is appropriately compared to the martial music.

Presently the cyclone blasts the hut. The poet's breath is suspended. From the shattered roof of the hut or from the sky dense drops erect the nocturnal dance. That is, it is already night. Or else densely dark clouds all over the blue deep have summoned the night in the day time only. The fleeting bubbles together raise pillars that dance. This is a unique imagery. Look at the solid wall before you. Is it not the dance of electrons? The poet can see the dancing water drops forming a column. When the roof of the hut is blown away by the cyclonic wind the vertical columns of incessantly falling rain seem to support the shack. Thus there is the hollow hut with pillars of fleeting bubbles. The columns are raised on the pebbles of the hailstorm. These are the imagery of the eye. Breathless however the poet listens. The waters falling on the pebbles of hailstorm liken the march of an army in battle array. The poet counts the minutes. Every minute is, as it were, an eon. And the march of the minutes is a kind of dingy dirge. Here dirge does not only mean a threat from military operation, it implies lament. It is dark all about. Darkness implies absence of all colours. When minutes are counted in this darkness dingy colours are perceived giving the impression of the appearance of phantoms. And lo! From the vacuum forged by darkness, from the deeps of the nihil, the dingy dirge or an inarticulate lament shows up and feels the void:

> Breathless I listen
> to the melting martial music,
> the passing away of naked minutes,
> a form of dingy dirge   (p.10)

'A Form of Dirge' thus distinguishes the poetry of Dr. Reddy. He is not a romantic. He does not agree with Shelley that if winter comes spring cannot remain far behind. True that spring follows winter. But a time might come when there will be no spring. There could be ceaseless winter. Does not the notion of entropy utter the self same truth? Reddy is anti-romantic after all.

The Cry

This is a poem packed with gunpowder of revolutionary thought. Revolt or rebellion is the result of endless cries of hunger. Earlier the poet has drunken deep in the fountain of sorrow and grief. This bitter potion in the poet's galled throat produced melodies in uneasy ecstasy. What is uneasy ecstasy or beyond oneself? The sage Valmiki while going to bathe heard the heart-rending cry of a krauncha, the she bird. Her mate was killed by a hunter while the birds were mating. This put the poet beyond or in ecstasy. In anger he thundered upon the hunter –'Oh thou hunter, you will never find peace and stability in life, because you have killed one of the mating birds'. God also cursed Cain on the same ground. And from this uneasy ecstasy of the sage Valmiki the epic poem *The Ramayana* flowed. Reddy recollects the episode in his inimitable style:

> From the death cry
> That pierced the heart
> When the hunting arrow
> Nipped the neck of a dove
> Emerged the immortal epic;   (p.13)

Just as the sky was loud with the cry of the bereaved female krauncha, so is the sky of our mortal existence loud with the laments of mankind. Valmiki lamented the death of the krauncha bird. He lamented the abduction of Sita. He lamented the death of Sri Rama.

Reddy, the Valmiki of our time, laments over numberless hunger deaths. Countless are our oppressed brethren and the cry of their agony is so deep and pathetic that it pierces the heart of every listener and seer:

> from the agonized cry
> of the oppressed brethren
> crushed between the grinding
> jaws of the greedy rich
> ushers the drum of dissent
> and the clarion of insurrection; (p.13)

The above lines can be considered a recordation of historical truth. In the recent past the French Revolution and Russian revolution are the terrible instances of blood-thirsty revolutions sparked by tyranny of the rulers and abject poverty and hunger of the people. This scorching is expressed by the poet in thought-provoking words. Expression of inner beauty which lies dormant in the core of one's heart emerges when the inner suffering finds at last an outlet. When it emerges is not known, but any amount of restraint cannot arrest its volcanic eruption. The spark of harmony which remains concealed in one's self struggles to find its external expression and when the inevitable moment comes it springs like a lotus flower from muddy waters. Injustices of the greedy rich provoke the people and one day or other all their sinful activities make the exploited sections to raise their hitherto suppressed voices and fight for justified rights. The general law or accepted truth is—every action is bound to generate an equal and opposite reaction. The reaction may not always be in an equal degree, but some reaction is bound to be there. That is why persons in power should ensure justice and strive for the well-being of all. They should not destroy people's trust and it is dangerous to play with destinies of people.

On the Death of Mrs. Indira Gandhi

This poem has something in common with the previously discussed poem though this is almost an elegiac poem on the death of Mrs. Indira Gandhi, the then Prime Minister of India. Mrs. Gandhi as shown in the poem is a powerful leader of the country and Dr. Reddy projects Mrs. Gandhi as a strong political leader just as the sage Valmiki projects his ideal leader in Lord Rama. Remember, Reddy projects her as a strong leader, not as an ideal leader because the poet knows that she could never be an ideal leader and it was she who had imposed Emergency in India during which period many national leaders of great stature were kept in prison. Dr. Reddy telescopes her political career. She was as it were a creeper in the shady support of the banyan tree. When the tree fell the creeper stood erect and gave shelter under its lush growth of leaves to all weeds, breeds, creeds and cults. Reddy neatly sums up her political career:

> Unconquered by pests that tried to foil
> till that fateful morn made all mourn
> when an ungrateful hand cut its span.   (p.32)

'On the Death of Mrs. Indira Gandhi' is a triumph of elegiac poetry. With all her defects she gained sympathy from all sections of people across the country with her unexpected death when she was at the peak of her career. The poet pinpoints her achievements that have been undone with her demise. She was -

> The beacon light of non-aligned nations
> Is extinguished in a sheet of curdled blood
> The torch bearer of disarmament summit ...   (p. 32)

Reddy speaks of her political achievements and is all praise to her political shrewdness which has made her one of the strongest leaders of the world. She was responsible for separating East Pakistan, for the creation of Bangladesh and for the consequent weakening of Pakistan. Her clever election slogan "Garibi Hatao' brought her close to the poorer sections. But all the same she had encouraged dynastic politics as well as corruption which Dr. Reddy criticizes on more than one occasion. He expresses his views on the present day political leaders in the very next poem 'Democratic Lines' which is a pen portrait of the present leaders. The poet knows with all her defects she was a successful leader of her period at the national and international level.

The Kite

Though pent up in a hut, our desires could excelsior and wing in the blue deep. Dr. Reddy externalizes this situation in the symbolic poem -

> Behold yonder in the sky
> The long tailed eagle sailing high
> Drawing brittle strength
> From a rainbow twig of little length
> And bonded life from a bundle of thread

> A flimsy bridle to its vagaries; (p.36)

Our desires draw brittle strength from the rainbow twig of our mind and of our being. The colourful kite of our desires is no doubt bonded by a bundle of threads. In one sense it is a pleasant kite and in another sense it is a swift-flying bird eagle. One of the threads is no doubt its love for the young in the nest which impels the skylark of Wordsworth the pilgrim of the sky to trace back its flight to its nest on the ground. Dr. Reddy reads a symbol in the Wordsworthian skylark myth. While Dr. Reddy's poem flies swiftly as a kite, and then enjoys a brief spell of rest viewing things below, Wordsworth's poem moves, to put in his words, in 'a rugged and an uneven manner' and we fail to find the swiftness of the skylark.

> It adorns the ethereal height
> with its thrilling fancied flight
> From the gross earthly base
> As an airy messenger of peace
> Borne aloft on the breezy palanquin; (p.36)

The moment the thread is broken the binding factor vanishes and the kite may fly for some time, but after some time it is bound to come down or it may get lost. Without bond of affection life goes astray as a kite with a broken thread. What a beautiful image! It works on different planes and different levels. But such bonds as love for the nest are brittle, hard but easily breakable. The bond breaks. The falcon thereby may not hear the falconer. Consequently it comes down or it is lost. Perhaps Shelley's skylark is the lost kite that floats and runs. It is no longer a bird but a blithe spirit whose race is just begun. But otherwise it could become a rudderless ship in the wide ocean of existence knowing not whither it goes. Then it would be -

> A tedious voyage
> without destination
> in dark stormy wind,
> gales and whales
> batter the tiny boat (p.16)

We saw earlier the hut as a metaphor of body or social ethos that provides us with a sense of security. A hut could be replaced by a boat afloat in the stream of time anchored in the social ethos of a time quantum and space quantum. But a storm shatters the anchor and tears the sail into shreds. In short the bonds are lost.

On one level when the kite is lost our desires and especially our desires for peace are shattered because of its wanton vagaries. On another level if the kite is identified with the self of the poet, a boat that has lost its anchor shaken by storm, the situation is different. We will come to that pivot of probability later. The kite lost is the unrealized dream of the common man. But the imagery of the kite is ambivalent. The kite might not be the messenger of peace. The kite going up could stand for the rocketing up of the essential commodities of everyday use shattering our hopes of reasonable living in economic plenty. The same kite might stand for our value judgments as it were. When the kite goes up our moral values and value judgments become nobler. But poet finds the kite coming down on the ground. In other words there has been a steep devaluation of our values.

Curiously enough when we see the upward flight of the bird as price rise of essential commodities there is devaluation in the economic realm. Consequently any downward flight of the bird might mean revaluation in the economic context. But from another context the upward flight of the bird could be the qualitative enhancement of our moral values and its downward flight might mean degeneration and devaluation of our moral values. Yes, that is where Dr. Reddy excels in creating a vivid and living scene and in focusing on the degree of depravity and in drawing our attention to the appalling reality. The kite fallen on thorny hedges is compared to the wailing woman who is molested by brutes who are the vultures alien to our noble culture:

> Kite, fallen and torn on the hedge,
> pensively recalls the wailing woman
> molested on the sacred soil
> by vultures alien to culture.   (p. 36)

When the kite touches the ground it indicates the fall of moral values which spells insecurity to women. In other words this is a world where no morality and value judgment breathes or exists any more. How prophetic the words of Dr. Reddy are! The lines prove Dr. Reddy at once a poet and prophet; when we look at the news papers and news channels no day passes without some gross injustice to women or horrible rape and murder in some part of our country or other which has compelled to the introduction of Nirbhay Law. More than 68,000 rape cases were registered during 2009-2011 while only 16,000 were convicted presenting a dismal picture of conviction of sexual offenders. The NCRB data shows there were 122,292 cases of molestation during 2009-'11, but only 27,408 could be convicted (www. First Post, Feb. 3, 2013). Number of rape cases has crossed the danger level and our national capital has come to be called as rape capital as there doesn't seem to be any safety for women there. Even the passing of death sentence for rape of minors doesn't seem to arrest such bestial acts. By using the image of kite fallen and torn on the thorny bush Dr. Reddy has succeeded in driving home the present helpless plight of women in general in India and the wailing picture of the molested woman stands before eyes. Thanks to the profoundly symbolical poem 'Kite' which runs at two levels, living and non-living.

When I Churned Time

The poem opens with the enigmatic line—'When I churned time'; though the speaker belongs to time and speaks at a time quantum and point, quantum stands outside time. Or else how can he churn time? He churns time with the toothed stick of his nebulous experience. Toothed stick is a weapon. The natives of Philippines have a piece of forged steel filed into saw teeth sandwiched between extra hard wood. When one strikes a thing with the stick, it not only breaks the thing it hits at, but also it rips the bones and muscles of the same. So when the poet churns time with a toothed stick he dares to hurt time to see its bones and muscles. This is an adventure singularly unique in the realm of prose and verse. The toothed stick is filed with the poet's nebulous or hazy experiences of life. Each experience of life looks like a sharp tooth of the stick. It hurts the poet when recalled. But the poet uses the same to hurt and churn time. In other words the poet forges a toothed stick with the experiences of his sufferings and churns time to see into time. The experiences are hazy because of the fact that they are bound to the uncertain future of the poet. True. The contingent world looks discrete.

But that is an illusion. Everything is tied to its unpredictable future. When we cannot speculate or imagine the shape of things to come, do we call the same death or *finis interitus* i.e. end by destruction? So haunted by uncertain future, the poet is troubled by heart-ache; it makes the poet imagine that someone close to him suffering from cardiac problem as mitral stenosis struggles gasping for breath. These are epic similes forged into a lyric. The poet, to repeat, churns time with toothed stick with great anguish at heart. The anguish precipitates into a potful of bitter potion. Thus while the churning is there without, it is also there within. The poet's heart is being churned when the poet attempts to churn time from without, because there is an invisible link between the world without and the world within. The subject is being influenced by the object of study.

Hence man is foredoomed never to study life as it is. He is always compelled to condition the object of study in his own light. If you want to find the speed of an electron you cannot locate it. If you want to locate an electron you cannot gauge its speed. And hence the usage of the term mitral-stenosis is rather ambiguous. As a matter of fact reference to mitral-stenosis seems to be entirely subjective as the poet's wife was found to be ailing with mitral stenosis in its initial stage which was later rectified by medical treatment. When I contacted the poet regarding the contextual significance of the medical term he explained the history behind the usage of the medical term 'mitral-stenosis'. That is, the orifice of the mitral valve is narrowed. Symbolically the poet can perhaps grasp only one aspect of what he probes into with his glassy eyes. This inability to grasp the whole import of time impels the poet to gasp for breath. The poet churns time.

At the same time his heart is being churned by his sufferings in life. From there the bitter potion springs. This is an ingenious interpretation of the churning of the ocean in ancient Indian mythology. The churning of the ocean in Valmiki's *Ramayana* implies the churning of the heart of the spiritus mundi with the nebulous experiences of the existence. And lo! There sprang *halahala* i.e. poison. In Indian mythology Lord Siva drank the poison to rid the world of its anxieties and groans. But the poet knows that he is not Lord Siva. He does not have the ascetic capability to drink death fullest or to the lees. But come whatever may, we are always at the receiving end and readiness for accepting the turns of fortune is all. So the poet states -

> I meekly accept
> my apportioned lot
> and glance with my glassy eyes
> the handful of my ashes
> generated in the process   (p.5)

While churning time and churning his own heart the poet finds a handful of ashes. In other words the poet in his mind's eye finds himself dead. This is a meditation prescribed in Tantra. The world in the contingent is as such made of the five elements air, water, fire, earth and space. The yogi imagines that he is dead and the water element in him such as blood mingles with the water element of the world; the fire element in him, that is the combustion in his body, mingles with the fire element of the existence; the earth element in his body viz. bones and flesh, mingles with the earth element and the space element in the body, that is the hollows in the body, mingles with the space of the existence and the breath of his body mingles with air. And yet he exists. He exists above the five elements and beyond the five elements. He exists beyond the cosmos of the senses comprising of eye and ear. As such the poet sees -

> the infinite particles
> swept off by the wild winds
> merge with the five elements.   (p.5)

This is a poem composed by a seer who is plunged into an esoteric meditation. Without spiritual experience it is not possible for a common poet to express such intricate thought which needs the ability of insight.

Chapter 5: Subjective Phase

In fact, Dr. Reddy composed his poems *The Fleeting Bubbles* during a period of life when he was terribly dejected. His beloved wife might have been in a critical state during this time. He remembers how his wife suffered at the hospital and how he watched that haunting night 'gazing at death/about to snatch my spouse':

> She struggled frantically for release
> Fighting every moment for breath   (I Am Tired, p.17)

May be when she was in the hospital Dr. Reddy had his first hand experience of a hospital. His poem 'The Hospital' may have been composed on this occasion. During her struggle for breath Dr. Reddy looked after her who was almost in the jaws of death in the hospital with sleepless eyes in piercing agony of uncertainty and apprehension. Conrad's Arshat was looking into the hopeless darkness of the world through the great light of cloudless day. Dr. Reddy saw night about to snatch his spouse in the eerily dark daylight. Sitting in tears by the side of his ailing wife Dr. Reddy ceaselessly prayed to the Almighty:

> To spare her from the icy touch
> Lest the young ones become orphans
> And frightened chicks driven
> By the mighty eagle through worlds
> Real and unreal, a ruthless race.   (p.17)

Thus the eagle we met in the poem 'Kite' here becomes capricious fate or time. God was kind at that time; however he turns deaf in the end. He did hear the prayers of the poet. Distress in life could be a blessing in disguise, because at the hour of deep distress we are drawn to God if any. And the poet's heart, at the moment of great distress, transformed into a cemetery, pensively overflowed with silent psalms.

At some period earlier to this, at an hour of deep distress the relatives turned away from the poet. Not only that. They caused much agony to him out of sheer jealousy and ennui. In villages sometimes it happens so and it is difficult for decency to exist. The poet says:

> My heart groans
> I see myself burnt unmercifully
> On the pyre of wounded feelings
> Which are crushed between the grinding jaws
> Of my kith and kin too selfish
> Deprived of grains of sympathy.   (A Forlorn Soul, p.9)

There is no limit for the sordid play of selfishness and it is well-known that when people are in need of some help they flock around their supposed saviour and as soon as their need is fulfilled they disappear and easily they forget the help and the one who helped. That is the way of the world and this selfishness has spread its wings to all spheres. Those who have received the help do not remain quiet, but soon they try to speak ill of the person from whom they have received the help. The noble man observes all this and this saddens his heart, but he does not want to show his sorrow or lament publicly though his feelings are wounded by the venom of the words of his kith and kin. Life is like this everywhere. The poet cannot even weep in public.

> Timid tears sink inside their refuge
> And dare not show their fluid face,   (p.9)

The poet is literally forlorn. He exclaims -

> With all my people around
> I am alone a forsaken man   (p. 9)

The poet knows the untold misery of the common people. He witnessed the terrible suffering of his wife. He is himself in great distress. He is like Lord Siva who drank the venom of life and existence. He seems to enjoy the hidden stings of ironical words of his fellowmen directed at him from all directions:

> I search
> for the dark shade
> beneath the sunny smiles
> of blooming petals of jasmine
> for the drops of venom
> that lie beneath the pot of milk   (A Search, p.29)

But the poet knows his limitations and says honestly that he knows he is not Lord Siva the God Omnipotent who swallows the poison in the creation so as to ensure life:

> I am no Lord Siva
> To swallow the halahala
> And save the universe
> Or save myself or my spouse   (When I Churned Time, p.5)

In that case is the poet under the spell of Thanatos or death instinct? Thanatos is at once replaced by Eros or zest for life. For a time the poet commands like King Canute:

> Tide
> Stop thy pride
> And foaming ride   (Tide, 14)

The tide could be time itself. The tide is here the tide of waxing grief, but neither the sorrow nor time could be stopped. A storm-blast has shattered the stay or the humble hut of the poet. Or else the anchor of the boat of life has been removed by the sudden storm. Storm leaves the boat in the middle of the sea. It is tossed by waves:

> Waves rise and fall
> Hope and despair   (The Tedious Voyage, p.16)

Still the poet cannot give up the journey. The little children are there. They must be saved in the jungle of the society where tigers and snakes and hyenas in the robes of men wait in hiding for prey. They must be saved in the wide sea of life from whales in human attire and gales which are the act of god. The poet says:

> Still I steer rudderless
> Gazing at the faint star
> Vainly hoping to come ashore.   (p.16)

Elsewhere he posits -

> I am alone, a desperate man,
> A lone one with a desperate will
> To drift the rudderless course
> To safe shores—a vain bid;   (A Forlorn Soul, p.9)

The marvellous sonnet "The Dark Valley" describes the predicament decked in different imagery. While rowing the boat the poet imagines that he faints and falls into the valley of night from the paradise of childhood when the way used to be smooth and clear. The headlong fall from paradise reminds us of the fall of Satan and his crew in Milton's *Paradise Lost*. But there was no fatal flaw in the poet's character unlike in Satan. Gods often torture us for sport. That is what Gloucester opined in Shakespeare. And mark the terrible sufferings the poet undergoes after the fall.

> The hair pricks the skull with the pins of adoes
> Oh! In the veins flows the bitter gall of woes
> It saps the thought and fells the edge   (p.15)

The words 'The hair pricks the skull with pins of pains' remind us of a crown of thorns. With Shelley in his early age to outstrip the speed of the West Wind scarce seemed a vision. With Reddy however to face the shafts of life was the pledge of early age. In other words while Shelley was aggressive in his imagination Reddy was defensive. While Shelley readily took up spears against a sea of troubles Reddy was decked in armour and shield ready to brave the onslaughts of the enemy that is existence. Just as Shelley fell upon the thorns of life so does Reddy faint and fall headlong into the valley of night—the encircling gloom that Conan Doyle saw in broad daylight. But unlike Shelley who would revolt against the decree of sporting gods, Reddy has moral courage not to rage and rant but to bear all the sufferings with infinite patience and stoic resignation ready to sip the cup of hemlock of life. He frankly tells us

> I am tired
> in the middle of life's journey
> In truth I am crushed
> Betwixt the grinding jaws
> of gnawing cares and disease
> echo of knell and distractions;   (I Am Tired, p.17)

In the poem 'The Wreck' the poet informs us -

> I clung to life
> like a shaded ivy
> or a mad lover
> that adores a strumpet;   (p.18)

Life is a strumpet i.e. life does not always favour the brave. Despite that the poet is mad of her. This love for life has inspired the pen of Dr. Reddy. But the ugly shapes and sounds of this strumpet life distract the poet. The world of the eye and ear ceaselessly draw us to the trifles of pleasures of life. The poet shuts his eyes in revolt against the alien invasion or distracting dust:

> Let the eyes be shut .....
> against alien invasion
> or distracting digital dust
> from the traffic-jammed roads
> of drunken dragons;   (Let the Eyes be shut, p. 6)

Reddy is thus a modernist poet who juxtaposes the sublime with trifle, hyacinths and biscuits. His style reminds us of Eliot:

> I have measured out my life with coffee spoons
> ('The Love Song of J.Alfred Prufrock')

Let us have the pleasure of comparing T.S. Eliot's line with T.V. Reddy's lines in the poem 'My Soul's Agony' from his first collection *When Grief Rains*:

> Forgive me, an unworthy self, my love!
> Far away I worship you in my pupil ....
> What did I to you? An unkind wretch!
> I measured you with sugar spoons
> And coffee cups. A cruel arithmetic! ....
> When shall I come to you to place
> the remnants of my heart at your feet?   ('My Soul's Agony', WGR)

There is spontaneity, there is the flood of emotion, intensity of intimacy, burning flame of penitential fire and loving humility—all rolled into one single whole. Can there be a better expression of man's love for the beloved wife? While Eliot's lines describe a worldly moment, Dr. Reddy's lines blaze with penitential fire; what a difference between the British poet and the Indian poet! Without an iota of doubt these lines of Dr. Reddy are as good or as great as the lines of T.S. Eliot.

In this context it is worthwhile to note a few line of his poem 'A Forlorn Soul' from the present book *Fleeting Bubbles* where he speaks of the state of his helplessness. He says 'I am alone, a forsaken man,/ a lone man with a desperate will/ to drift the rudderless course/ to safe shores'. He says in the earlier lines his perception of the situation at that time is not clear and often it goes wrong. He needs recharging of his spirit; there is sincerity. Nowhere does the poet indulge in the art of speaking falsehood; indeed it is a great virtue for any poet:

> My eyes are gnawed by aberration
> Blindness alone is divine sight
> Timid tears sink inside their refuge
> And dare not show their fluid face.   (p.9)

Once the eyes are shut the poet cannot be distracted anymore from pleasant illusions by elusive delusion. The poet wants to breathe in his make-believe world. But the poet cannot escape from the world of senses by shutting his eyes, because he finds himself like a frightened cat below a creaking cot with rolling illicit lovers. What is that? That is the poet's shadow. In the own words of the poet -

> My dark shadow
> Chased and engulfed me
> Made a captive of my substance
> In tense flight and fright.   (In Tense Flight, p.7)

The shadow is the carnal desire lurking in the subconscious mind. The legitimacy is clear. If we try to escape from the world ridden with desires and objects we cannot get at freedom. So Reddy suffers and this he expresses as he is honest to the core. The world is as it were a closed door room wherefrom there is no escape. It puts in our mind absurd dramas.

When a particular cause of grief is found to recur everywhere in the life of everyman, the grief loses its edge. Reddy smiles and says— 'meek suffering has become my badge' (p.15). The badge of suffering suggests that the poet is done with his sin. Henceforth the will of God and not the poet's own desire shall direct his life; and surely when the poet posits that there is no bridge to cross the maze of misery, consciously or unconsciously the poet alludes to Indian philosophy. With Indian philosophy this world is a maze of sorrow and one must avail oneself of the bridge to cross the maze of sorrow and reach nirvana. But the poet laments — 'In vain I grope in the dark to catch a beam of light.' (p.15).The poet finds himself tossed on the waves of hope and despair. Sometimes it appears that the poet is half in love with easeful death. He seeks venom that lies beneath the pot of milk. But the next moment he searches for the ray of constant hope behind the halo of moonlight. To toss with the waves of hope and despair is the destiny. Think of the Indian bride:

> The rising waves and stormy gales

> Of the Bay of Bengal pale here
> ...
> Hopes fill her mind like summer showers
> Soon fears settle like monsoon clouds; (p.2)

Agony

The lines of the poem are present the state of mental agony of the poet who conveys his agony in an oblique way. We have already dwelled on how deeply the poet felt at the imminent death of his better half. The poet's hut was battered and shattered by hailstorm. He was banished from his surroundings. He availed himself of the boat. The boat was thrown into middle of the sea by storm blast again. Alone in the boundless sea, the poet has been singing dirges that have no ending. This is the melancholy voice from exile that we hear. Fighting every moment for breath while rowing, face to face with death, the poet can survey the whole of life ranging from birth to death. Every birth is as it were the outcome of a horrid duel and the world appears to be in total darkness frantically searching for a ray of light. Everywhere there is anarchy and even the midnight hour which should be one of silence is in reality unruly with unlawful activities raising their ugly heads. Lack of clarity and cleanliness in the modern world is reflected in the lines of the poem where the meaning gets concealed in loud conspiracy and our attempt to arrive at the correct meaning ends as an abortive coup. In the furious game of lust and sex man comes to grips with guilt only to die on the Ides of March:

> In this unruly midnight
> Two stainless steel knives
> Full of rust to the heaving hilt
> Have come to grips with guilt
> In lustful fury and agony;
> Strangely a moment ago
> They cozily enjoyed
> A common sheath, a slut
> that did not mind the split;
> the sharp razing friction
> and the forced tear on the wall
> The razor sharp edges
> Continued in mute mutiny,
> Nay in loud conspiracy,
> Pierced through the womb

An abortive coup, an operation.   (Agony, p.11)

It is a vivid description of sex battle in unruly midnight actuated by lustful greed and agony and a description of c-section. It is said that Caesar was born in this way. The *Suda*, a 10th century Byzantine Greek historical encyclopedia of the ancient Mediterranean world, states - when his mother died in the ninth month they cut her open and took him out[2]. Every child is born through great care. Every mother could die while giving birth. The poet imagines that a great warrior like Caesar must have been born with armour. But every child is born with a priori protection. Every child is a Caesar destined to achieve conquest. But every child including Caesar has to die on the Ides of March the destined day of one's exit from this stage. No one can avoid death. Death seems to be preordained:

> Retirement from the chair or stage
> is a certainty—a worn out truth;   (The Teacher, p.24)

And a person who knows that the exit from the stage is inevitable leads an authentic life according to Kierkegaard. And one is apt to ask—What is death? On one level it means the dissolution of the body into the five elements. The flesh and bones merge with the earth. The heat of the body merges with the fire element. Blood and phlegm merge with water, breath merges with air and empty spaces in the body merge with the space or *aakaash*. The visionary poet sees—

> The infinite particles
> Swept off by the wild winds
> Merge with the five elements.   (When I Churned Time, p.5)

One asks—is that all? Is there nothing called mind? What becomes of mind? Well, that is a pertinent question. Reddy is at once a poet and a prophet. But we will try to retrieve the answer from Reddy's poems to such questions a little later.

Before dwelling on death we had better understand what life is in Reddy's light. On the surface, the temporal space between birth and death is called life. We are born into the society and the world. We have already seen the society through the eyes of Dr. Reddy where women go with empty pitchers. The average Indians among whom we are born have no past and no future:

---

[2] www.mentalfloss.com/article/50179

> Days without memories and without dreams
> Are like empty pathetic pitchers;   (Memories, p. 34)

As the 'Birthday Party' shows the rich and the elite in the society are also thoughtless. They are sans love and compassion as well. Such ugly shapes and sounds tell upon the poet. The poet says 'I am tired'. But just because he feels tired he does not want to escape from the field of life. He intends to see the various phases and colours of life, analyze all these aspects carefully and then arrive at a synthetic understanding and evaluation of life. His approach to life is not divisive, but it is holistic.

Belgium Mirror

Reddy sees his shadow on the mirror. When he looks at the Belgium mirror he sees his reflection which is quite common and natural, but on this occasion he sees beyond the reflection and finds multiple faces of his one face split into so many. For a moment he could not understand himself or his person which is an indication that often we fail to understand ourselves and when we can't understand ourselves how can we understand others and think of evaluating others? This aspect of psychological truth which people do not like to accept finds a beautiful expression in the poem 'Belgium Mirror':

> This morn the dazed razor
> Gazed at my gaping face
> A hairline cut with peeping blood
> Lo I looked straight
> into the Belgium mirror
> Aghast I saw my defaced face
> Hewn into thousand crumbs
> picked up by winged cannibals
> all the hair had fled aloft
> the skull transformed into bowl
> beyond the hope of plastic surgery
> with insensate fury I dashed it
> all the pieces mocked at me.   (p.12)

When I shave with a razor the razor undoubtedly shaves me. When I look at the performance of a razor, the razor being dazed also gazes at me. This is Foucault's gaze. If we gaze at anything it gazes at us in turn. And both the doer and the agent find a hairline cut with peeping blood. The poet or the doer now sees his face on the Belgian mirror. It is a magic mirror that reflects the shadow or the subconscious of the poet. What does the poet see there? Thousand crumbs are picked up by winged cannibals. This is surrealistic imagery that benumbs our conscious minds and makes us aware of the threshold between the conscious and unconscious mind. Thousand crumbs of our face seem to be picked up by the thousand winged cannibals such as hatred, jealousy, cruelty and myriads of desires. It reminds us of the aesthetics of cruelty of Antonin Artaud.

With insensate fury the poet dashes the mirror that mocked at his real face lurking behind the apparent face. Appearance and reality is a recurrent imagery in Reddy. In the human world as experienced by Reddy -

> Smiles conceal the stabs
> As perfumed coffin the corpse.   (p.27)

Here we are reminded of the famous line of Shakespeare: "One may smile and smile and still be a villain!" How true the words are! In the same breath Dr. Reddy expresses a universal truth with an equally powerful image of the perfumed coffin. But one wonders, should we not be reconciled with the ambiguity of the existence? After all life is not a bed of roses and the picture of life can't be uniformly rosy; it is a mix of joys and sorrows. That is why at one moment or other every person becomes a Prince Hamlet speaking to himself or herself - 'To be or not to be, that's the question'!

> Is this world so beautiful?
> The rose has its thorn
> Jack has its prickles   (p.27)

The face is zoomed. So what is not visible in the face to the eye ordinarily is distinct and clear when the face is zoomed. We could say the face is bloody like the apparition of Banquo's ghost. May be the poet feels he, in other words his sum of values, has been killed by the Macbeths of our time spiritually with the aid of assassins. But when the poet says the razor itself has caused the cuts in the poet's face while shaving it could have different connotation. If one's face is ripped or lacerated while shaving, one is responsible for one's misfortunes. On another level, razor puts in our mind the profound thought of the Upanishads. The Upanishads observe -The path of God-realisation is as horrendous as the razor's edge:

> Uttishtata, jagrata, Prapyavaran Nibodhata
> Kshurasya dhaaraa nisitaa duratyayaa

Durgam pathastat kavayorvadanti.   (*Kathopanishad*)

And may be the poet while on his spiritual journey has fallen on the razor's edge. The poet has chosen the path that is as fierce as a razor's edge. In fact journey along the razor's edge likens a tedious voyage in the midst of the blue deep, the roaring and racing waves, steering rudderless knowing not which way to go, vainly hoping to come ashore. But again the poet points out that his face is hewn by winged cannibals. What are winged cannibals? Are they the unlawful forces in the society? Are they seconds and minutes and hours? Do they allude to Time?

'When I Churned Time' and 'Memories'

Though the former poem has already been discussed separately, it needs to be dealt afresh along with the latter poem. These two can be read as companion poems. While rowing the boat of life the poet churns the unfathomable sea and unfathomable time with the toothpick or toothed stick of his nebulous experience. Yes in the eleventh canto of the *Bhagavad Gita* God reveals Himself as Time personified. And lo! Whatever has been created by time and whatever waits to be created by time is chewed and devoured by Time. Anyone who wants to recollect the past must retrieve their traces dangling from the teeth of Time. Hence poetic use of the toothpick or toothed stick has its functional significance. Anyone who seeks to know what is in the cards must churn time with toothed stick. Life is made up of the past and the present and these two lead to the future; without being aware of the past experience with all its delights and defects one cannot shape the future. Generally the course of future depends on the past and the present. To know the yesterday and to guess the tomorrow makes life what it is:

> Without yesterday without tomorrow
> Today has no life nor meaning.   (Memories, p.34)

When a child is born everything is probability. When it grows and becomes a man the past has been a necessity, but the future remains a probability. Life is indeed a queer sequence of events where the past seems to possess some logical necessity, but the future remains a probability. Life is thus a queer thing juxtaposed between necessity and probability. The seer in the poet comes out in the philosophical understanding of the concept of time which is entirely an abstract one synthesizing the three apparent classifications of past, present and future. In fact time past and time future find their inseparable unity in time present. Dr. Reddy's lines in turn remind us of T.S. Eliot's memorable lines on time in his long poem *Four Quartets* a philosophical treatise.

When the churning of ocean is there both manna and hemlock could be extracted from it. But the lot of the poet was decreed otherwise. It is *halahala* or hemlock apportioned for the poet. And the poet says:

> And I meekly accept
> My apportioned lot
> And glance with my glassy eyes
> The handful of my ashes   (When I Churned Time, p. 5)

Earlier we saw the poet heroically taking up arms against a sea of troubles. He was ready to drift a rudderless course to a safe shore. But now it seems that catharsis has taken place and there is the calm of mind. This is perhaps the predicament of every Indian. Every one is a tired or a tireless sailor in the foaming sea of existence.

In this context the first eleven lines of 'When I Churned Time' are significant. Let us have a look at the lines:

> When I churned time
> With my toothed stick
> of my nebulous experience
> twisted with the thin rope
> of my uncertain fate
> bubbles of heart aches
> sprang spasmodically
> precipitating pejoratively
> into a potful of bitter potion
> incarnating into mitral-stenosis
> that made me gasp for breath.   (p. 5)

The poem with all its seeming simplicity is deftly woven with contrasting threads of obscurity which makes it a complex one with a hard layer. The philosophical concepts of time and fate are introduced on one side and on the other medical terms such as 'mitral stenosis' and 'spasms' (connected to tetanus) are used. It is the juxtaposition of the personal and universal elements that invests the poem with its unique aura of aesthetic sensitivity.

The poem 'Memories' is in a sense thematically linked with the above poem and as such it can be read as its companion poem. Memories are appropriately compared to glowing candles that lead us with the required light in our journey. Memories refer to our past scenes, situations and activities covering successes and failures, contributions and disappointments while dreams refer to our desires and aspirations to be realized. After some time 'dreams may recede, but their shadows linger'; moments of joy may pass on, but their pleasant memories definitely remain in our mind often visiting and re-visiting. The poem closes with the two lines packed with universal truth and philosophical as well as practical meaning -

> Without yesterday, without tomorrow
> Today has no life, nor meaning.   (p. 34)

Any act of knowing must negotiate with the unknown. That which cannot be anticipated must be taken into account in the light of experience. Without yesterday and without tomorrow life has no meaning. Yesterday implies memory. Since the present or today is different from what we experienced in the past there are the past and present. In the past men would protect women. But nowadays the women are ignored. It is through difference that both the past and present exist. It is this difference that constitutes memory which brings diverse zones together. The past exists only through the lens of the present. The past and the present are not two discrete notions. Each one is constitutive of the other. And time is not a linear progression. That is why the poet churns time with the tooth pick of nebulous experience. Time is neither wholly present nor wholly absent and it is evanescent like fleeting bubbles and any experience that constitutes time or that is constituted by time is nebulous. T. S. Eliot observes:

> The memory throws up high and dry
> A crowd of twisted things
> A twisted branch upon the beach
> Eaten smooth and polished
>   ('A Rhapsody on a Windy Night')

A non-linear and discontinuous twisting of language speaks of the nonlinearity of memory. And mark you, neither the yesterday nor the tomorrow or the uncertain future is present. Juxtaposed between the two absences what is the true nature of the present? Is it not a fleeting bubble? But the present of the poet is the inevitable necessity. It has erased our, what Halbwachs would call, collective memory.

> Days without memories and dreams
> Are like empty pathetic pitchers.   ('Memories', p.34)

Have we not already seen women with empty pitchers? They have neither dreams nor memories. Memories are like glowing candles. No wonder the women of our villages look like expiring candles. He is in exile, because honesty is in exile. But at the same time he feels that he could be separated from the soul of his soul. Even if one is alienated from the society one is not really alienated, but when one is alienated from the soul of one's soul one is alienated.

'My Soul in Exile' and 'A Miracle'

The poet is already in exile as we know. He is an exiled soul groaning in the prison of the world whence there is no respite or escape. He is as it were on a tedious voyage without destination. The only prop and support is his lady love who is undoubtedly his beloved wife. His wife is the source and spring of inspiration for his creative muse. The company the lonely poet has is this affectionate lady without whom his Muse will not shine. And now follows a hymn to the beloved lady who is the source of his Muse:

> Don't quit, be with me
> My prop in stress and strain
> Let us sail or sink together.   ('My Soul in Exile', p.19)

In the hour of stress and strain it is this lady in whom he finds his prop and it is her timely compassion and everlasting love that saves his sinking soul and recharges his weakened spirit. Without her sunny smile he cannot produce the melodies of his verses and his lines would virtually become dry and sterile; it is her smile that makes his creative spirit bloom and blossom. Her graceful presence elevates the poet to a height of ecstasy and without her he was bound to be uneasy; and when the mind is uneasy how could he produce melodies? Most probably it is the critical condition of his lady love which is at the root of the poem. In an hour of deep distress inwardly he prays to God not to alienate her from his life, from this world. He identifies his joys and sorrows with hers and he finds his life in her existence or death in her end.

And surely at this stage a miracle happens. The poet's lady love who is at the point of passing away resurrects under the spell of the poet's genuine love in its purest form. With a resurrected hope the poet now instils the potential seed of the revived hope in the heart of his lady love who recovers from the serious illness or crisis. His love for her is so deep and true that he finds a new spring after the painful stretch of the wintry autumn. He consoles his love who intensely feels and weeps for the dire misfortunes that the poet suffers. As an ideal lover or husband he does not want to see a single sorrowful tear in her eyes and any trace of sorrow in her heart would make him miserable and rends his heart in twain. As a loving husband he wants always to see his wife in smiles and finds his bliss in his perfect union with her:

> Don't weep my love
> A tear from your eye
> Tears the leaf of my life
> Rends my heart on twain
> Be unmoved of my state
> Though you see
> The stream of tears
> Flowing from my eyes
> They are not tears of sorrow
> Pearls of peerless bliss
> of our affirmed union
> You almost a fallen leaf
> Are now green and fresh
> Spring has come again
> A surprise? A solace?
> Or a miracle!   ('A Miracle', p. 30)

The poem is unique. In the whole range of the poems of *The Fleeting Bubbles* love songs are not there. We have been helpless witnesses of the critical moments of the health of the poet's wife. That was the moment of losing the paradise. When she recovers, as though by a miracle, and resurrects in the shape of the poet's Muse there is paradise regained. The poet unites with his Beatrice, his Muse and at once spring comes to him. The poet asked earlier -

> How long shall I hide
> This bitter potion
> In my galled throat
> And produce melodies
> In uneasy ecstasy
> With my soul in exile?   ('My Soul in Exile', p.19)

The soul has returned to the poet. The rapture resulting from the union with the soul is seldom experienced in English poetry. This poem is unique in the sense that it gives us the feeling of the ineffable joy of regaining the rapture of conjugal paradise. When most of the renowned poets of the post-independence period celebrate the hunger and thirst for sex defiling the pages and the minds of the readers, it is indeed a welcome change when a true poet Dr.T.V. Reddy celebrates conjugal love and yearns to find the peerless bliss in their affirmed union and his paradise in the love of his wife.

Chapter 6: General Phase

The basic needs of a citizen include food, shelter, clothing, health care, utilities and education. Think of the housewife who hesitates to kindle the hearth and feeds her stomach with fond hopes of blank future. Think of the old woman. Her stitches in sari outnumber the wrinkles in her face and body. For all the risks a snake charmer courts, he gets a handful of rice. And look at the old woman. She sits on the hard but hospitable stone for decades. According to 2011 census 15 percent of the people in India are homeless. A tsunami or a flood could make one homeless. The poem 'In the form of Dirge' gives a first-hand description of what it is like to be homeless being cyclone-blasted. But the cyclone blast could be a metaphor. There could be a family disaster, separation, unemployment, riot, disease, drug addiction that may act as a tsunami and it could render man homeless.

When the home is breaking down every naked minute is hard. And to be homeless is to steer across the sea of life knowing not where to go braving the tides and storm blasts. This is not due to the want of wealth. This is due to the mal-distribution of wealth. We have seen how the cry of the very baby whose birthday is being observed gets buried beneath the dunghill of thrown away leaves and tipsy looks. Thus there is the plethora of plenty side by side with chill penury in our country. Robbed of their home and robbed of their work which could distract from distraction and gnawing pain and gloom, these homeless people are neo Bedouins of the capitalist system. In ancient days Bedouins were the nomadic Arabs of the desert. And a day might come when the neo Bedouins, offsprings of the unequal distribution of wealth might rush in hordes knowing not whither to go and destroy the much vaunted civilization of ours. Perhaps Spengler would support whole heartedly the premonitions of the poet Reddy.

Dr. Reddy alludes to Valmiki. Valmiki saw a hunter killing a bird that was engaged in mating with a she-bird. The wails of the she bird filled the sky and provoked Valmiki to utter a curse on the hunter.

And that was the origin of the epic *The Ramayana*. Like Valmiki Dr. Reddy also curses the hunter. The hunter here stands for the greedy rich. Dr. Reddy is capable of forging cruel imagery. In the poem 'The Cry' we see the rich people grinding the poor crushed between their jaws. We can hear the sound of grinding the poor, just as the hunter killing the bird provoked the curse of Valmiki:

> 'Maa nisada pratisthaam tvamagamah shasvati samaah
> Yat krauncha mithunaadekamavadhih kamamohitam.'

In the context of Dr. Reddy's poem the meaning can be construed approximately as –'Oh Hunter! You will never have a home that is sustainable. Since you have killed one of the pair of romancing birds so will the laments of the dying masses usher the drum of dissent and clarion of insurrection.' Let us have a look at Dr. Reddy's lines:

> Springs the volley of thunderbolts
> And rise the potent spark of revolt
> Whose flames kiss the sky
> And reduce life to ashes
> From which phoenix rises.   ('The Cry', p.13)

The flames that kiss the skies might remind the reader of Dido's funeral pyre. Is Dido the symbol of love and chastity, the symbol of the hungry millions whose hearts long for love and grovel in the dark dying once again? But Reddy knows that from the ashes phoenix rises. Thus Reddy is the incarnation of Shelley as it were who believes that if winter comes spring cannot remain far behind. Humanity, the staunch optimist Dr. Reddy believes, will resurrect like a phoenix even if the whole earth is turned into a vast necropolis. Here one is reminded of the words of Albert Einstein: "I know not with what weapons World War III will be fought, but World War IV will be fought with sticks and stones." Man is playing like monkey with atoms. If there is another nuclear war man shall have to fight with sticks. With Dr. Reddy that is the rise of the phoenix from the ashes.

In fact all this is the consequence of the economic system prevalent in a country. And it goes without saying that the economy of a country depends upon the political system of the country. No wonder the word economics as such is a misnomer. Political Economy is the determinant of the economic state of the country. And what kind of politics is in vogue in our country? The poems 'Democratic Lines' and 'In Exile' give a vivid picture of politics in India. The poet describes the nature of the sudden rise of politicians. From which walk of life do the politicians come in India? A drop-out in the school, a black marketeer, a matinee idol of the masses, a racketeer or a gambler could be a politician. They take advantage of the illiteracy or greed of the masses, caste and communal emotions and buy their votes with money as well as false promises, because they are liars. They have neither control over their words nor do they have control over their mind. They are fleshy leaders trading in flesh. This is reminiscent of Dryden. In *Absalom and Achitophel* Dryden describes the physique of the politicians. Their figures are eloquent about their self-seeking nature. The behaviour and performances of the modern pot-bellied politicians puts in our mind the *rajadharma* as delineated in Vidur-neeti and *rajadharma* of ancient India. *The Mahabharata* Shantiparva chapter152 states that the chief duty of a king is to enact sacrifice and Gift. He should perform acts of compassion. He should study the Vedas. And to speak the truth is usual with him:

> yajno daanam dayaa vedaa satyancha prithivi pateh
> panchaitani pavitraani shastham sucharitam tapah.'

Besides the above five duties the kings should lead a pious life and revel in penance and pious austerities. So a gambler or a matinee idol does not deserve the power of a ruler. King Dasaratha chose Rama as the crown prince, only because the people wanted him to be the king of Ayodhya when Dasaratha would retire. King Dasaratha wanted to make his subjects happy—'*prakriti priya kaamyayaa*'. As people wanted Rama to be the crown prince, so he elected, While in so-called democracy people are being cheated by their elected rulers, even when kingship was in vogue will and not force was the basis of the state. Consent of the people was a must for a king to rule.

'The Democratic Lines' however tells us that we live in a state which is *araajaka* or lawlessness where there is no good governance. Scandalised with the misbehaviour of Duryodhana, the son of the king Dhritarashtra of Hastinapur in the great epic *Mahabharata*, the wise and honest Vidura went off to exile by choice and joined the Pandavas in the forest for a time. How could Vidura describe his situation in a dramatic monologue? Perhaps we could put the poem entitled 'My Bare Needs' in the lips of Vidura:

> Enough, enough
> I want nothing
> I ask nothing;
> .....
> My hunger migrated

> to the white fields
> while my bare needs
> get blasted by iconoclasts;   (p. 26)

How did Duryodhana respond to the situation? To speak in the words of Dr. Reddy -

> Hypocrisy climbs atop the ladder
> And reigns supreme in seer's garb
> Mocking at honesty in exile.   ('In Exile', p. 28)

One of the great points of excellence in Reddy is that he is so steeped in the time-honoured Indian values that unaware of all this, his poetry alludes to the ancient Indian scriptures and ways of life. Herein lies the secret of the greatness of his poetry and its compelling appeal with its irresistible melody to our minds. In fact the natural flow of melodic line is Dr. Reddy's unique contribution to Indian poetry in English.

Now if there is the introspection of the self in the poem 'In Exile', the poet looks at his own face on the Belgium mirror in the poem of that title. Belgium mirror is very truthful to what it reflects. In more than one sense the poem 'Belgium Mirror' is a triumph of poetic art that invokes Mandelbrot. When Mandelbrot went to measure the coast line of England he found it to be infinite and apparently it has metaphorical link with Reddy's symbolic line –'a hairline cut with peeping blood'. But when the poet minutely observes his face on the glass he feels frightened to see his defaced face:

> Aghast I saw my defaced face
> hewn in thousand crumbs
> picked up by winged cannibals;   (p. 12)

Then the poet psychologically feels that he is in a state of exile or simply he finds himself in exile. In this metaphor of exile what is perceivable is the feeling of alienation. The expression 'defaced face' involves deeper psychology and strikes a discordant note appropriate to the context; in one sense it means we are not what we are and we are not what we look. In other words it is a clash between appearance and reality which requires a deeper study in relation to the present social life. It is a subtle reference to modern man's split personality. The poet rightly feels he is alienated. The extraordinary creative power in him finds expression in subtle ways:

> The cobra the vanquished captive

> With a stony glitter in its lidless eyes
> Hissing in vain with vengeance
> Raising his dreaded hood
> With all its mortal fangs removed.
>
> (The Snake Charmer, p.25)

This is alienation in the sense of paucity of power. The individual's faculties and behaviour are of no avail to reinforce what one seeks. We are simply powerless snakes with all the fangs removed, conducted by an indeterminate social force or who knows by Fate. Think of the bride gaudily dressed like a doll:

> She is content to be his slave
> Ready to play to his whimsical tunes
> And pay heavily for the dear prize.   (p. 2)

There is alienation in the sense of meaninglessness. When the sensed ability to control outcomes fails it is powerlessness. Failure of sensed ability to predict outcomes is meaninglessness. An instance of this type can be seen when the women of the village -

> They turn homeward with pitchers
> And wait for their men
> With flickers in their eyes.   (p. 1)

Or else when the housewife -

> .... waits with a wick in her eye
> for her partner from the furrowed field.   (p.23)

It is alienation because of meaninglessness. Then there is the alienation because of anomie. It speaks of socially unapproved behaviour to achieve given goals. Reddy observes:

> But our professed leaders
> Professional dissemblers
> ...
> Catch people's vote
> with spurious currency notes   (In Exile, p. 28)

Familial estrangement also leads to alienation. Reddy exclaims:

> I see myself burnt unmercifully
> On the pyre of my wounded feelings
> Which are crushed beneath the grinding jaws
> Of my kith and kin too selfish

Deprived of sympathy. (A Forlorn Soul, p. 9)

And the sad state of self estrangement has inspired the poem 'Belgium Mirror' which we have dwelled on presently.

And then there is alienation from the self. It is the consequence of being a mechanistic part of a social class estranged from humanity. How mechanistic the elite class is in its behaviour pattern is best described in 'The Birthday Party':

> Hands shook smiles expanded
> Lips lisped while candles blinked
> Glasses clanked to the loud beauty
> Of the bangles of show case dolls
> Amid dance and caresses   ....   (p. 4)

Both Shakespeare and Reddy have two loves, one of comfort and another of despair. Reddy's Dark Lady is Life itself:

> I clung to life
> Like a shaded ivy
> Or a mad lover
> That adores a strumpet,
> But lot of filth
> She flung on me
> A heartless jade;   (The Wreck, p. 18)

So we have already seen that the poet Dr. Reddy symbolically has two loves, one of comfort and another of despair. On the face of it the persona gives the impression of being infatuated with the love for life. Life is a strumpet. It does not favour the brave. It fills the path of life of the brave and the courageous with insurmountable hurdles and riddles. One who has the right to an honourable life is deprived of the laurels. Life does not have any pity for the poor and the destitute, the deprived and the deserving. A battle awaits him every moment in every plan and in every move in this game of chess which is life. Despite that the poet is infatuated with life. He clings to life like an ivy creeper or a mad lover. The ivy-mantled tower resounds with the knell of the curfew announcing impending death. The poet exclaims:

> 'I fear—a sad merry fear
> She may engulf me;'   ('The Wreck', p. 18)

Life is the *la belle* sans mercy. It is as it were the boa constrictor. We know that it will kill us. But like a drug addict we cling to her. The oxymoron in the phrase—the merry fear describes eloquently the

Catch 22 situation of Everyman under the sun. The poet says: 'She may engulf me'. The poet is himself the Everyman, enamoured of life. Life seems to engulf the whole of humanity. The lust for life seems to generate an impending flood that will drown and down raze everything noble and majestic and beautiful that has decked the history of man. Selfishness, greed, consumerism and the mad race for market with their aftermath in war between nations characterize the lust for life. Humanity met such dire situations in the past as well. The myth of a great flood destroying everything recurs in the Puranas littered all over the globe. But as the Bible narrates, God the Father gave a command to the pious Noah to build a mighty ark that might save the chosen few from the raging waters of the media-loud roaring waves of lust. But alas, this time the enchanting deluge seems to have wrecked the globe and cracked Noah's ark. Indeed the earth is the only spacecraft where man could inhabit during his sojourn from life to death. But it has been cracked and despite that the poet cannot get rid of the mortal embrace of Life.

The poet fled away from the Dark Lady i.e. Life. What is Life? Life is everything encompassing all that includes you, me and all. But in his flight the poet found himself like a frightened cat under the cot creaking with rolling illicit lovers. The poet could not run away from himself. The shadow of its material self chases him and engulfs him. True the material self could be destroyed by life. In a vision the poet sees with glassy eyes the handful of his ashes generated in the process:

> 'And see the infinite particles
> Swept off by the wild winds
> Merge with five elements.'   (p. 5)

Fire, air, water, earth and ether are the five elements that constitute our body. 'Dust thou art, To dust thou returneth.' But does the poet pin his faith on utter annihilation? Does the physical death of a person mean utter annihilation of the person? No. With the poet:

> 'When time rings the final bell
> Unawares we make our exit
> From the stage without a sign.   (p. 8)

The word 'exit' here is significant. When Shakespeare told us that the world is a stage for man, it seems that he did not believe in the annihilation of a person. Similarly Reddy also does not look upon death as annihilation. There must be some substance in the person which is not made of the dustiness of dust. Yes, Reddy believes in that substance which is not dependent on anything else but itself. With Reddy, shadows make a captive of the substance. In other words, he seems to speak of the soul which weapons cannot tear, fire cannot burn, water cannot wet and air cannot dry as declared by Sri Krishna:

> "Nainam chhindanti sastraani, Nainam dahati paavakah/
> Na chainam kledayan tyapah, Na soshayati marutah." //

Reddy feels that this soul is a captive in the rose mesh of flesh. What are shadows but the multitudinous lures of the world of Maya? Man finds himself bound by the chains of *maya* and as long as he is under the grip of *maya* there cannot be any release; in other words he cannot hope to have *mukti* i.e. deliverance. The world of shadows has been deftly delineated in 'The Birthday Party' where artificiality reigns:

> Glasses clank to the loud beauty
> Of the bangles of showcase dolls
> Amidst dance and caresses (p. 4)

Reddy comments on the nature of the party which is an offshoot or an imitation of western culture resting on outward show and superficial values:

> 'Ashes of haunting status lingered still
> Vainly attempting to arrest the cycle
> And imposed stasis with benumbed fingers'. (p. 4)

If the transmigration of soul is believed in, the shadows or the lingering ashes of the haunting status could be read as *Samskaras*. The word *samakara* has an extensive multi-layered meaning with deeper connotations stretching to the previous births. It is the collective result of the essential character, influenced by so many factors connected with this birth and the previous births deriving the nucleus of strength from the *vasanas* descending from previous births as an invisible force. In general context one can consider it an equivalent of the term culture. The poet asserts that the flux of life does not cease with the departed soul. The soul departs but does not die. It might change the body impelled by the *samskara* but it knows no death. So when the poet fears that life or his lady love might engulf him, one might say that the poet is scared of being ever rolling in the tedious and tiresome merry-go-round of life and death and rebirth cycle. Is there no way out?

The poet sees himself on the Belgium glass. He finds how he has been battered by the harsh pranks of life. The poet finds himself unmercifully burnt on the pyre of his wounded feelings which are crushed by the grinding jaws of his kith and kin. Consequently the poet has lost his eyes and lost his ears i.e. the sense of right perception. The poet himself cried—'let the eyes be shut'. At another place the poet asserts that he has the right to blindness. Because as we know Tiresias the blind could see more than Oedipus who had his eyes open. The poet shuts his eyes and shuts his ears and shuts all the casements of the sense organs. And now the poet introspects. He becomes aware of the mind and the deciding force of *sraddha* the seminal element that strengthens the mind. Without sraddha life is of no use and it is sraddha that shapes one's life and decides the destiny of man or woman. This concept is expressed in the remarkable poem 'The Mind' which seems to have been inspired by the unforgettable sloka of the *BhagavadGita*—'Yoyat sraddah sahevasah' which means 'Man is what his *sraddha* is'. Truth is not there in the world of the senses. Truth is not there in the world of the contingent. The world is surrounded by illusions and is full of speculations and the spark of truth is covered by the embers of illusions, wild surmises and glittering laces of false notions and conclusions. On the contrary -

> Mind is the laboratory
> that discloses the laws of truth
> amid illusions and speculations;
> it solves the insoluble
> when rightly directed   ('The Mind', p. 35)

But who will direct? Where is the preceptor or the Guru?

> The purohit performs the rites of Agni
> while they see the borrowed currency in flames.   (p.2)

And again in the poem 'An Old Woman' -

> 'The swamiji saw her (old woman) on his way, spat at her went in fury for his ill luck to see her first'.   (p. 21)

So the Guru cannot be found in a temple or in a church. The poet wants the inner vision. Where is the Dorothy who gave Wordsworth his eyes and ears? Though Dorothy was the sister of Wordsworth, did not the poet descry the shooting light in her eyes? Reddy's Dorothy is not in the world without; she is in the world within. She is the love of comfort. She is the teacher and the preceptor of the poet. But as soon as the poet is aware of Beatrice, he feels that he is not united with her. May be she has quit the poet. And Reddy's 'My Soul in Exile' is a marvellous love poem:

> 'Don't quit my love
> Without you why should I live
> And lose my identity
> In the prison of a world'   (p. 19)

A man can assert his identity in the prison house of the world only when he is accompanied by his wife and beloved. The Vedas assert that the offerings to the fire should be performed by both the husband and wife together, because both wife and husband together can give a sense of completion to any sacred act and their united prayer alone can yield rich dividends and richer fruits on the spiritual plane. But nay, our true wife is our deeper consciousness i.e. the purer mind and not the love of comfort which is related to the physical body only. Once one is away from the purer mind, one becomes mad and a wreck. One becomes a doleful lover of life that is a strumpet. Far away from the self of the self, far away from the love of comfort, the poet's throat has been galled and he has produced melodies in uneasy ecstasy with his soul- the Beatrice, the Dorothy away and far off.

Chapter 7: Spiritual Phase:-

Dr. Reddy is so steeped in spiritual consciousness that it is seen as an undercurrent running in his poems. The subject may be secular or spiritual, the treatment may be to a large part in consonance with the subject, yet each poem can be seen shining with the golden lace of spirituality. Whether it is the Indian bride or the hospital, flux of life or churning of time, the cry or the tide, an old woman or snake charmer, death or democratic lines, mind or kite, lotus or jasmine, almost every poem breathes the aura of spiritual fragrance either directly or indirectly. The thought of the Supreme God is the basis for the framework of Reddy's poems, whatever may be the theme. The last poem 'The Supreme Being" is totally steeped in spirituality and it proclaims the all-pervasive nature of the Supreme God. Reddy gives expression to the great Upanishadic thought which is universal above all the narrow limits and boundaries of diverse creeds, religions and faiths.

This spiritual atmosphere can be felt right from the opening lines of this book when he presents the peepal tree by the side of the pond near the village; in other words nature i.e. *prakriti* the visible power that stands for the invisible force of God who is the Omnipresent One without the second is presented in its three-dimensional manifestation. Peepal tree is the Aswattha tree referred to in the Upanishads and in the *Bhagavad Gita* as well. The Universe is symbolically described as the aswattha tree with its root upwards and all the branches, sub-branches and leaves growing and looking downwards. Dr. Reddy in the opening poem 'Women of the Village' presents 'the pale peepal tree' where the word 'pale' symbolically refers to the weakened spiritual values; with the dilution of spiritual values waters of the pond gradually decrease and a stage may come when the pond becomes totally dry.

All our Hindu scriptures reiterate that in a kingdom where the king protects *Dharma* i.e. morality and where moral values are preserved that country is blessed with rains and it will prosper and people will be happy living in peace. In poems 'The Hospital' and 'I am Tired' the poet calls the Supreme God as the great Healer and in times of crisis even the priest or purohit prays God the Protector to save the person from the critical illness and situation. Sri Aurobindo in the beginning pages of his famous spiritual epic *Savitri* in Canto I (p.3) writes—'All can be done if the God-touch is there.' When everything is said and done one is aware of the fact that ultimately it is He who decides and this spiritual truth is echoed by Dr. Reddy in all his writings in some form or other.

The poet's strong faith in the Sublime God finds its expression in almost all his poems. In the poem 'Flux of Life' he refers to God as Time and it is most appropriate that He is personified as Time, because it is He who governs Time and to His supreme vision there is no division of time as past, present and future as they are a single unity. That is why Lord Siva is known as Kaleswar or the Lord of Time at the famous Ujjain temple and daily the puja commences with a unique form of worship by praying with ashes freshly brought from a burning pyre at the burial ground. It indicates the Lord is the Lord of Time, the decider of our life time and ultimately the Lord of Dissolution of all life and non-life, animate and inanimate, in the Universe. We do not know anything about our entrance and exit; it is He who decides our birth as well as the end. The same God, Kaleswar the Destroyer, is referred to Lord the Protector in the poem 'When I Churned Time' where the Lord swallowed all the poison i.e. halahala' to save all the living world and preserved it in his throat in order to preserve all life from death. We may call God with various names and describe Him as per our wishes and fancies, but they all refer to one and only one single God the Creator.

While the poem 'A Form of Dirge' begins with the line 'While the Zero hour/ of the cyclone-blasted hut' and describes 'the passing away of naked minutes', the very next poem 'Agony' starts with the line – 'In this unruly midnight' and presents the birth and death of Julius Caesar: 'Caesor is born with armour/to die on the Ides of march'. These are all direct references to the omnipotence of Time, the image of God. The voice in 'The Cry' is a direct reference to the Supreme God the supreme character in the ancient epic *The Ramayana*, while 'Tide' is an indirect reference to the Omnipotent which sees the fall of pride and power. History abounds with numerous instances of monarchs, ruthless rulers and dictators and invaders such as the mighty Alexander, the ruthless Ghazni, Chenghiz Khan, Timur, Alauddin Khilji, Aurangazeb, Nadir Shah, General Dyer, Hitler and many others who all, having conquered many kingdoms and causing the flow of streams of blood and laid many kingdoms to ruin and wreck and waste, bowed at last to Death the Lord of Time.

The 'beam of light' in the beautiful poem 'The Dark Valley' and 'the faint star' in the piece 'The Tedious Voyage' are clear references to the Supreme from a desperate soul. When a person is surrounded by difficulties and sorrows he naturally thinks of the Lord and at one moment or other prays for the grace of God; it is human nature and it is an undeniable fact. The helpless old woman in the poem of the same title is a clear example when she prays the Lord to save her from all the ignominy by taking her to His world i.e. by granting her instant death.

Spiritual thought dominates the presentation of the teacher (p.24) who is placed along with God. Sanatana Dharma insists that teacher should be treated on par with God; in fact he is ranked a step before God as teacher or guru is to be worshipped as 'Acharya Devobhavah'! Of course in ancient days teacher was a *rishi* or a sage with spiritual knowledge or he was one who had attained God-realization. The lines are ever quotable:

> If the Almighty creates, he re-creates
> And transforms the raw substance
> into a refined one, rich and noble;   (p.24)

The lines of the poem 'The World beautiful' refer to unlimited variety in the creation of the supreme God as the world is full of dualities; joys and sorrows, thorns and flowers, teachers and traitors, the poor and the rich, the fair and the foul coexist—that is the inherent wonder of God's creation. While in the poem 'In Exile' integrity and honesty stand for God, hypocrisy and depravity stand for anti-God. Poet's spiritual bent of mind is discernible in the lines of the poem 'Then and Now' where Dr. Reddy makes use of the Biblical words Adam and Eve. Even the lines of the political satire 'Democratic Lines' bristle with spiritual aura when Dr. Reddy describes the present day corrupt political leader sarcastically as 'the self-styled saviour'. The poet knows that God alone is the Saviour while these corrupt leaders pose as if they are our saviours. Both the poems 'Memories' and 'The Mind' have the glow of spirituality. While the former ends with the concept of Time, the later deals with the spark of spirituality and ennobling soul:

> Mind becomes rich
> with an ennobling soul
> the immutable image

of the supreme being. (p. 35)

The essence of spiritual knowledge can be felt again in the poem 'Lotus' where the blooming lotus is referred to as the blossoming soul. The term 'soul' though it generally signifies Atma, is rich in meaning; and as we find in *Bhagavad Gita* though Atma means the Supreme Soul it sometimes refers to mind, sometimes to intellect and to individual soul or the Jivatma. Paramatma dwells seated in the thousand-petalled lotus of our heart and ultimately the spark of life departs from the crown or top of the head through what is called Brahmarandhra.

One of the finest heroic poems in world literature depicts a situation where gods were dispossessed of the heaven. Consequently they assembled at a valley in the Himalayan range and chanted hymns invoking the blessings of the Mother goddess so that they could regain the sway over the paradise and other worlds. While they were plunged in chant and meditation, a little girl was passing in their neighbourhood. She asked the gods—'Whom do you pray?' At once a body leaped forth from the body of the little girl and proclaimed that the gods were worshipping her. In fact mystics testify that there are bodies within the body. Alcott the theosophist speaks of the astral body. Hindu philosophy posits that there are five sheaths—the *annamayakosa* or the food sheath, *pranamayakosa* or the vital sheath, *manomayakosa* or the mind sheath, *vijnanamayakosa* or the wisdom sheath and the *anandamayakosa* or the sheath of bliss.

Vasudeva Reddy speaks like a mystic as well by referring to lotus. He speaks of two loves. One is associated with Tellus or the earth. The other is associated with Cynthia or the moon. Flanked between two loves T.V. Reddy our Endymion being enchanted with the phenomenal world was separated from his love who speaks of the beyond. Yes there was a time when the latter, as it were, was about to quit the poet. And the poet burst in a love song praying her not to leave him. The love for worldly life or Life pertains to *annamaya kosa* and the flesh of the poet. The other love, the love of comfort pertains to *manomaya kosa* or mind sheath. So both the loves, one of comfort and another of discomfort, do belong to the self of the poet. So the poet is aware of more than one self in him. And he prays to the inner self who is drifting away from the poet. And lo! A miracle takes place.

The poet finds his inner self in tears at the love of comfort. When we men are drawn to the material pleasures our inner self weeps out of dejection. But we the average rung of men are not aware of that, but the poet is different. Like the ancient philosophers and the rishis, he has perceived that the comforts of the phenomenal world might be sweet for a time but bitter in the long run. Think of a party or a function and beneath the seeming waves of pleasure there is an undercurrent of grief:

> Beneath the surging smiles of guests,
> pomp and pageantry, glitter and feast,
> flows the eddying stream of her parents' tears;   (p. 2)

When he tries to look at the wheel of time and tries to churn time with his nebulous experience he realizes his limitations and he knows that 'I am no Lord Siva/ to swallow the '*halahala*'/and save the universe/ or save myself or my spouse'. He meekly accepts his apportioned lot; in other words he is always aware of his state. Humans, however great or powerful, are fleeting bubbles and their existence itself is brief and they have to bow before the call of the Supreme Being by whatever name It may be called. Here in the phenomenal world all that glitters is not gold:

> Smiles conceal the stab
> As perfumed coffin the corpse.
>   ('Is the World Beautiful?', p. 27)
> …
> The drops of venom
> Lie beneath the pot of milk;   ('A Search', p. 29)

Here in the world there is the wide gulf between appearance and reality and one cannot be carried away by the appearance though it may look beautiful and attractive. In this context we are reminded of Shakespeare's oft-quoted lines: 'Fair is foul and foul is fair'- with which the play *Macbeth* begins. Now look at the lines of Dr. Reddy:

> The wolf in ass's hide
> A hoarder in the hermit's guise
>   ('Democratic Lines', p. 33)

Our physical body could be likened to a boat. Often we identify our self with the body or the boat. And the journey of the boat along the sea of the boundless phenomenal world is -

> a tedious voyage
> without destination
> in dark stormy wind
> gales and whales   ('The Tedious Voyage', p. 16)

Thrashed and pummelled by the phenomenal world the poet shut his senses and lost his senses. In a vision he saw how the body belongs to the material world. He saw the reflection of his lacerated face on the mirror. But that is external self. He broke it into pieces. He had shut his eyes only to look upon his eyes. Thus he started observing himself. According to the *Brahmasutra* one who observes himself is god. Thus the poet is aware of a self within the self which is not material subject to destruction. And once the poet went inward he saw his lady love of comfort was as it were parting just as the Rajyalaksmi or the Prosperity of a kingdom often takes to her flight. But in fact the inner light or the lady love of the poet, the self of the self, never parted from the poet.

The poet himself said that in the direst situation of his life when he was carried by the storms of life to the middle of the sea without any direction he was determined to steer the rudderless boat gazing at the faint star. Did not Ulysses make up his mind to follow knowledge like a sinking star? Reddy's poem 'The Tedious Voyage' explicates the imagery of sinking star. The sinking star is the faint star of Reddy. It is the lady love of comfort who was about to go away. But the poet's eager request to her—'Don't quit'—brought her close to the self of the poet. She has tears in her eyes because the poet had ignored her earlier. And the poet consoles her -

> Don't weep my love
> A tear from your eye
> tears the leaf of my life
> rends my heart in twain;   ('A Miracle', p. 30)

Reddy also breaks into tears. Tears of the two lovers, the self of the poet and the inner self of the poet, in embrace forge a sacred confluence where lot of energy of love and compassion can be seen. We readers gaze at it awe-struck and bathe in the confluence. The two together now delve the mind where the poet gets a hunch of the super-conscious, because with the spark of spirituality mind becomes the super-conscious. With the inner eye the lovers gaze at the super-conscious—the everlasting and the eternal. This is just the opposite of the fleeting bubbles and the evanescent. It ignores the transitory. Minds, enriched with the experience of the Supreme Being at the level of the super-conscious, the two lovers, in fact the two selves of the poet, in the presence of the Supreme Being have their lovely whispers beneath the jasmine bower that showers flowers and fragrance on the pair. They remind us of the Blessed Damozel bathing in the well of light before the eyes of mother Mary. This is transcendental love and amour rarely found in the so-called love poetry.

Now the poet is back to the world of the readers and the worldly life and chants in ecstasy in the spiritually significant poem 'The Supreme Being' which is an expression of the sublime thought. The deep impact of the Upanishads and the *Bhagavad Gita* on the mind of the poet can be seen in profusion in every line of the poem and the entire poem is steeped in the essence of Sanatana Dharma which has its profound impact on the poet. In fact we feel as if we are reading a divine song or psalm expressed by a devotee in a mood of ecstasy:

> In the blooming petal of the flower
> I behold the smile of the almighty ....
> In the awesome sight of the roaring billows .....
> And in the terrible beauty of the snake
> I hear the breath of an unseen force
> Formidable and inscrutable in nature
> In the midst of deep mystery around me
> I feel the grace of the Supreme Being.   (p.39)

Now the poet is more or less a realized soul—a rishi of the Upanishads who has reached a transcendental state where he beholds the omnipresence of the Supreme Lord everywhere. A man with a sense of realization alone can give expression to the above thoughts packed with spiritual essence. A person steeped in spiritual contemplation beholds the spiritual force or spark in everything animate or inanimate, because everything in the universe owes to Him as He is the Creator. To reach this stage is not easy; unless one has a deep sense of spirituality one cannot develop such a spiritual frame of mind.

No wonder when the poet sees the Supreme Being both in prosperity and adversity or in every misfortune of life one cannot but ponder over the Omni-presence of the Supreme Being and yearn for the honey of His bliss and peace and divine grace and in such a moment of ecstasy he cannot but rap out -

> Madhu vaataa ritaayate
> Madhu ksaranti sindhavah
> Madhu dyau astu nah pitaa
> Madhumat paarthivam rajah."

This can be translated as -

> The wind is blowing honey

Honey oozes forth from the ocean
The skies and our Father are honey
The earthly dust is also honey.'

Chapter 8: Conclusion

Indeed the poems of *Fleeting Bubbles* have been harsh melodies in uneasy ecstasy. We have seen the women stand like expiring candles. We have heard the wedding music and wedding bells that sound the knell of the evanescent happiness of a virgin. We have espied the senior nurses in white robes behave like white elephants and new-hatched doctors pruning their plumage like young Chanticleers in the hospital and our elected leaders totally corrupt. We could hear the cry of the baby on the damp bed getting buried under the dunghill of the parrot words and patent sounds when the birthday of the very crying baby was being observed. Our future is uncertain. Our eyes are being invaded by distracting dusts from the traffic-jammed roads and so on. The unique quality of this poetical work, though slender in terms of quantification, is it is at once a social and spiritual work embracing all the aspects of social life, exposing the hitherto unexpressed problems and sufferings of peasants and tribal folk, farmers and rural folk and the artificiality inherent in egoistic lives of the urban folk as well as the limitless greed of political leaders always indulging in cheating and corruption in the guise of lucrative democracy.

May be the death in life of the Indian masses has driven Dr. Reddy to pen the melancholy notes in this remarkable poetic work *Fleeting Bubbles*. Just as the laments of the female krauncha bird prompted Valmiki to chant the first verse in the language, so the agonized cries of the people between the jaws of the self-seeking rich spurred our poet to portray fleeting bubbles. But the poet hears in the cries the inarticulate drum of dissent and the clarion of insurrection and articulates this cry in such a way that it echoes even in passive minds and stirs even the indifferent hearts. His poems have the ingrained power to move and stir the hearts and his lines are prophetic. When Valmiki's curse thundered in perfect poetry Brahma the creator showed up before him to make him compose the story of Rama. Similarly Dr. Reddy's dirges lamenting the lot of the masses and the sorrows of existence seem to have united him with his Muse.

And now the poet looks inward. Earlier in prayer he was as inert as a cemetery. In other words he was as it were in Samadhi state. Listless of the happenings in the world without, the poet was plunged inward. Now he explores the mind. Truth is not there in the world without. It is only in the secret niche of the mind that one can detect the truth rid of all illusions and speculations. With us the future is probability. But if one can discipline one's mind with patience, the future is in the living present. This is why, Valmiki, who observed penance for ages together to discipline his mind, could see into the veil of future of Lord Rama when he was only in his prime youth. Mind is the seat of the super-conscious. Dr. Reddy has described the phenomenal world as fleeting bubbles only in relation to his inner life that is strongly built on the granite foundation insoluble against the ages because of penance. Penance disciplines the mind. Once the inner eye opens, the ennobling soul, the immutable image of the Supreme Being, the everlasting and the eternal, is revealed before it. At once the sorrows of life seem to be fleeting bubbles sans any substance. What is the soul like? The *Bhagavad Gita* says:

> Weapons cannot tear it, Fire cannot burn it,
> Water cannot drench it, Wind cannot dry it.

This wonderful poem unlocking the untold treasure and potential of mind reminds us the first verse of Dhammapada:

> Manopubbangama dhamma[1]
> manosettha manomaya
> manasa ce padutthena[2]
> bhasati va karoti va
>
> tato nam dukkhamanveti
> cakkamva vahato padam.
> *Manopubbangama dhamma*
> *manosettha manomaya*
> *manasa ce pasannena*
> *bhasati va karoti va*
> *tato nam sukha[1] manveti*
> *chayava anapayini."*

Mind is the forerunner of all phenomena. Mind is the greatest of all the senses. Everything is made of mind. If one speaks or acts with polluted mind sorrow follows him like the wheels that follow the bullocks. If one speaks or acts with happy and contented mind happiness follows him just as a shadow follows a person and he is never separated from happiness. Look at the lotus. Lotus is born in the mud of existence. But it smiles in serene joy floating above the waters. It picks out the pearls from its leafy platter. Thus the poem reminds us of the Mahayana classic *Lotus sutra* or *Saddharma pundarika*. Lotus is also thus the type of the poet who culls the archetypes from the platter of collective mind. The poet also perceives:

> The unfolding petals
> As many as the hurdles
> That lie across life's journey
> Bloom like the blossoming soul;   (Lotus, p. 37)

This imagery in a flash drives us to reconsider the past journey of life which seemed to be laden with sadness and untold sufferings in a fresh light. Moreover the poet's skilful use of the word 'unfolding' in its continuous form is very much symbolical suggestive of the continuing hurdles in the journey of life without any break or stop. In fact the poet's journey was from without to within. Now that his inner eyes are open and now that he can have a glimpse of the Supreme Being all those hurdles of yore seem to him to have been transformed into the opening petals of bliss. So let us welcome each rebuff that makes the smoothness of the path of life rough. The rishi of the Upanishad chants -

> Uttishtata jaagrata praapya varaan Nibodhata
> Kshurasya dhaaraa nisitaa duratyayaa
> Durgam pathastat kavayoh vadanti."

This can be translated in the following words that can approach the original to the nearest possible degree:

> Arise, awake and get at your goal.
> But mind you—The road is as sharp as razor's edge
> The seers say the path is too tough and it is a difficult journey.'

Do we not remember how the razor cut the poet's face in thousand pieces? The poet fell on the road that is as sharp as the razor's edge and his face was cut into thousand pieces. Thus rising from mud and blood the lotus begets pure beauty.

> Likewise soul encapsulated in a body
> Sheds slime and mortal coil,
> Soars to the ethereal heights

>   And loses identity in the eternal.   (p. 37)

Thus *The Fleeting Bubbles* ends with the chants of the Upanishads. It reminds us that every man is but a living soul in mortal coils. In course of our journey in quest of eternal stay we have to brave the hurdles of life which will cleanse the slime and the mortal coils of existence so that unburdened and light we can excelsior to the Supreme Soul in whom we will pour into and vanish. The sufferings of life seem to us as insurmountable as crossing the boundless sea in the night. But the title of the book of poems tells us that they are fleeting bubbles. Yes the fleeting bubbles are the godhead in myriads of fragments that rise and pour into the Supreme Soul. So what seems transitory is not transitory but part of the eternal. What seemed painful is not painful but part of the eternal bliss. And hence we can chant the Upanishad again:

> The dust of the earth is honey
> The wind that blows is honey.

And in this transformed atmosphere alive with the fragrance of jasmine flowers we find man and woman—a newly wedded couple have their lovely whispers beneath the jasmine bower that showers flowers on the pair. Earlier the poet shot a sharp shaft of satire at a wedding party. But now the poet blesses them and is delighted to see them in delight. The jasmine bower showers flowers of benediction upon every lover and his beloved. But this is not carnal love. It owes nothing to Cupid or Jove. It seems as it were Dante and Beatrice or Rossetti himself and Rossetti's lady love are sitting protected in a jasmine bower embalmed in the fragrance of the jasmine flower. And these visions are living truth with the poet. So in the last poem 'The Supreme Being' the poet clinches up his sequence of fleeting bubbles with the indelible impression of the Eternal without which nothing exists. The poem with all the lines steeped in spiritual essence reminds us of the lines of Wordsworth (from his popular Ode *Intimations of Immortality*) who sometimes looks at simple things with an inner eye and feels the all-pervasive impact of nature which is a living spirit to his poetic vision:

> To me the meanest flower that blows can give
> Thoughts that do often lie too deep for tears.

While writing on the recollections of his early childhood Wordsworth expresses that during that early stage all earthly things and common sights such as meadow and grove, rose and bird, wind and stream, rainbow and the moon, did seem to him 'apparelled in celestial light' in all their freshness and glory. He felt the fullness of bliss and the soul rising in joy, God as their home and that 'Heaven lies about us in our infancy'. The same feeling is expressed in T.V. Reddy's end poem 'The Supreme Being'. In the fragrance of the flower, in the terrible ceaseless roar of the ocean, in the deafening sound of the dark thunder, in the hissing of the poisonous snake, in the movement of tiny creature, in everything animate and inanimate and in the deep mystery around him he feels the breath as well as the grace of the Supreme Being.

Moreover the conception as well as the structure and texture of the spiritual thought of the poem reminds us of the supreme thought of the Upanishads:

> Purnamidam Purnamadah
> Purnaat Purnamudachyate
> Purnasya Purnamaadaaya
> Purnameva avasishyate."

This illuminating Sanskrit sloka, a treasure house of spiritual and scientific truth with its boundless spiritual light, means:

> This is full, that is full
> It is from the full that the full springs
> If you take away the full from the full
> The Full alone remains.'

Thus *The Fleeting Bubbles* ends in benediction. That is why to an ordinary academic mind Reddy's poems at first glance may seem as laboured products, but to a higher intellect steeped in ancient Hindu thought with poetic instinct his poems are indeed spontaneous expressions of higher inspiration yielding rich ancient Indian thought and spiritual essence that are often out of the reach of a common mind. His poems, though apparently simple, demand a careful and serious reading to get a taste of the concealed layers and latent treasures of deeper meaning and universal truths. In him one can find the spontaneity of British romantic poetry, the rhythm of Sanskrit sloka and the natural music of his mother tongue Telugu hailed by the Europeans as the Italian of the East. The spontaneous flow and natural music of the lines makes his poems readable quite a number of times and with their universal appeal most of the lines richly deserve to stay green in our memory. This is a great virtue of Reddy's poetry which distinguishes itself from the poetry of other Indian poets in English.

Though he comes in the post-Emergency period the significance of his poems rises above the imaginary boundaries of block periods hypothetically erected by our scholars and critics of narrow vision. As his poems reflect human nature with basic feelings and sentiments they have acquired universal significance and as such the relevance of his poetry transcends limitations of time and place thereby acquiring the lasting virtue of durability. Moreover his poetry stirs our minds and compels us to reflect and there are many quotable lines that richly deserve to stay in our memory which fact distinguishes Dr. Reddy from other poets who have come after Independence. Rejuvenated with a fresh zest for life the poet as well as we readers could resume our journey of life after an hour of introspection.

OM SANTIH! OM SANTIH! OM SANTIH!

Appendix 1: The Fleeting Bubbles – Complete Text

THE FLEETING BUBBLES
(A Collection of Poems) by T. Vasudeva Reddy
(Pubd. by Poets Press India: Madras, April 1989)

Foreword by Dr. Georges C. Friedenkraft

(Dr. Friedenkraft is a Poet & Critic based in Paris, France).

Throughout his successive works like *When Grief Rains* and *The Broken Rhythms*, T. Vasudeva Reddy was adhering to a lyricism falling halfway between reality and the imaginary. Reality is certainly evoked as the constraints and sufferings of the world are not alien to the poet while he bears witness to his time, his burdens and his hurts; and the imaginary also since poetry is dreams of another world and the transposition effort of changing evil into pure gold.

The present work is a smooth prolongation of this poetical dialectics. The world, and of course notably India, are ever present—the emergence of old age, existential fatigue, emergencies at the hospital, the death of Indira Gandhi, the rejection of the widow, the disappearance of the wife. More than ever, as compared to his past works, the author involves us in the difficulties of being and becoming:

> 'I am an old woman with the help of none'
> ....
> Her arms were bare with blistering boils
> Her face, brow and breasts were all wrinkles ....
> (An Old Woman)

But if from the cries of pain born from hunger, from 'the agonized cry/ of the oppressed brethren ...' springs 'the potent sparks of revolt', poetry, since it is dreams, could transform the revolt and its embers into dreams. Thanks to poetry, love with its tenderness and blossoms could still triumph through the armour of the rude happening.

> Jasmine is soft, serene and pure
> Offering wondrous balm of cure

> For those profoundly in love …. (Blessings of Jasmine)

And finally the poet rediscovers, beyond his worldly sufferings the smile of the Supreme Being:

> In the blooming petal of the flower
> I behold the smile of the Almighty   (The Supreme Being)

It is not possible to give an outline of the work in a few lines. Only the reader could allow himself to appreciate the qualities, the power of suggestion from the images, the impact of words, the harmony of rimes and alliterations and, above all, the intense feeling which vibrates from each verse. Dr. Reddy's poetry is richly lyrical and imagist, and what is more remarkable in his poetry is that it at once suggests and stimulates. His poems that deal with human themes show his utmost human concern and the intensity of his feeling heart; at the same time, in a subtly satirical and ironical vein he lashes at the injustice, social or otherwise.

Earlier I have said that the poet is a witness of his time and also a messenger of dreams. Dr. T.V. Reddy is a fine example of such a poet. His poetry transcends the bitterness and the gall which mark our sojourn on this earth. May he help mankind to close down the house of tears and go and live amongst the 'blessings of jasmine'!

Dr Georges C. Friedenkraft
Paris, France

(Adaptation into English from wan Hua Goh-Chapouthier)

Fleeting Bubbles **Contents**

Women of the Village 117
The Indian Bride 118
The Hospital 119
Birth Day Party 120
When I Churned Time 121
Let the Eyes Be Shut 122
In Tense Flight 123
Flux of Life 124
A Forlorn Soul 125
A Form of Dirge 126
Agony 126
Belgium Mirror 127
The Cry 128
Tide 128
The Dark Valley 129
The Tedious Voyage 130
I Am Tired 131
The Wreck 132
My Soul In Exile 133
A Widow 134
An Old Woman 135
The Corn Reaper 136
The Housewife 137
The Teacher 138
The Snake Charmer 139
My Bare Needs 140
Is the World Beautiful? 140
In Exile 141

A Search 142
A Miracle 142
Then and Now 143
On the Death of Mrs. Indira Gandhi 144
Democratic Lines 145
Memories 146
The Mind 146
The Kite 147
Lotus 148
Blessings of Jasmine 148
The Supreme Being... 149

Women of the Village

Beneath the pale peepal tree
by the fast drying pond
in that double roasted hamlet
women stand like expiring candles
      Passively they fill
        their empty earthen pots
        bending like famished cattle
        that drain water to the lees
The clear water moves
in concentric circles
like their day dreams
      Catching snaky visages in water
      weaving desire in the plaits
      of their cobra-long hair
      they carry pots of sweat
Covering staring breasts
with their sari-ends
they turn homeward with pitchers
      and wait for their men
      with flickers in their eyes.

The Indian Bride

Amid vaunting faces of kith and kin
concentric circles of friends
she is alone in solitude
sitting by the winking groom.
As mute as an adorned idol
in an overcrowded temple
she sits depressed, a mind agitated;
dressed in gold-laced Kanchi silk sari
adorned with stone-studded jewellery
she looks like a bedecked doll In a show case
or a vanishing species in a zoo.
The rising waves and stormy gales
of the Bay of Bengal pale here.
The contours of her heaving bosom
draw the E.C.G of her uncertain fate
to be shared by an unseen face;
Beneath the surging smiles of guests
pomp and pageantry, glitter and feast
flows the eddying stream of her parent's tears;
the Purohit performs the rites by Agni
while they see the borrowed currency in flames;
wedding music charms her heart
though drained by traditional ills;
Hopes fill her mind like summer showers
soon fears settle like monsoon clouds;
The triple knot of 'thali' around her neck
shining symbol of new bondage
mocks at the thrice-cursed bride.
Having bought the groom in auction
as cattle dealers buy their lusty bulls,
she is content to be his slave
ready to play to his whimsical tunes
and pay heavily for the dear prize.

The Hospital

The case remains the same
No change in patient's condition—
The chief doctor burning a cigar
with decades of decadent experience
gives his Delphic oracle
after a fortnight's senseless stay
in the I.C.U. of the Emergency ward
All tests are conducted
diagnosis seems to reach its destination;
treatment continues round the clock
for the probable disease,
still an enigma baffling their brains;
Nine-tenths of their knowledge
assumes it to be a type of tetanus
while the remainder suggests meningitis;
still a fraction roams in ambiguity
a larger cloudy canvas, the nebula;
Some nurses treat like real sisters
while their seniors in white robes
behave like white elephants
A few new-hatched doctors
wear airs pruning their plumage
like young Chanticleers
winking at the studious steths;
The priest prays at bed-side
the Great Healer for speedy recovery;
On the road of trial and error
one quizzical drug cures the patient
and drowns the profession in wonder;
At last they pride themselves
when the disease, the vanquished victor,
walks majestically with another prey
in search of a fresh contract.

Birth Day Party

Mike thundered the Pandal
a bowing miniature sky
bright with the flood of mini-bulbs;
fleet of cars blocked the street
drowned in gales of bizarre music;
sophisticated shadows flocked the hall
to celebrate the birthday
of the bed-wetting child;
hands shook, smiles expanded
lips lisped while candles blinked
glasses clang to the loud beauty
of the bangles of show-case dolls,
amid alien dance and caresses
the east and the west debauched;
The cry of the baby on the damp bed
got buried beneath the dunghill
of thrown-away leaves and tipsy looks
the parrot words and the patent sounds;
soon the chiming chorus receded
leaving a void infected with the notes—
many happy returns of the same;
ashes of haunting status lingered still
vainly attempting to arrest the cycle
and impose stasis with benumbed fingers.

When I Churned Time

When I churned time
with the toothed stick
of my nebulous experience
twisted with the thin rope
of my uncertain fate
bubbles of heart aches
sprang spasmodically
precipitating pejoratively
into a potful of bitter potion
incarnating into mitral-stenosis
that made me gasp for breath
I know—I am no Lord Siva
to swallow the *'halahala'*
and save the universe
or save myself or my spouse
still I meekly accept
my apportioned lot
and glance with my glassy eyes
the handful of my ashes
generated in the process,
and see the infinite particles
swept off by the wild winds
merge with the five elements.

Let the Eyes Be Shut

Let my eyelids
close or seal themselves
in intensive intercourse
or mute myopic mutiny
against alien invasion
or distracting digital dust
from the traffic-jammed roads
of drunken dragons;
let the eyes be shut
lest they should be distracted
from pleasant illusions
by elusive eerie delusions.

In Tense Flight

I fled away
from you, from me and all,
I thought so; but alas!
I found myself amid you
like a frightened cat
under the creeping cat
of rolling illicit lovers;
Could I run from myself
No, my dark shadow
chased and engulfed me,
made a captive of my substance
in tense flight and fright.

Flux of Life

My heart is bowed down with grief
The dread of the deceased dear
haunts the mind awake or asleep
more so in grave solitude
Loneliness intensifies sorrow
None accompanies the dead
however dear they are
unless the summons come;
Flux of life doesn't cease
with the departed souls;
though they make their exit
stream of life flows on
in full current for the rest
to swim or to be swallowed;
We should have some work
to distract us from distraction
or from cancerous greedy ulcer
and to dispel the clouds of gloom;
Work lessens the gnawing pain
by making time fleet and race
for unknown Time alone can heal
the woes and throes of the heart;
When time rings the final bell
unawares we make our exit
from the stage with a sigh.

A Forlorn Soul

My heart groans
I see myself burnt unmercifully
on the pyre of my wounded feelings
which are guilefully crushed
between the grinding jaws
of my kith and kin, too selfish,
deprived of grains of sympathy.
Liver thus roasted with gridiron
on the sparks of flaming greed
appeases their fastidious tongues.
My eyes are gnawed by aberration
Blindness alone is divine sight
Timid tears sink inside their refuge
and dare not show their fluid face
The hand that served as a prop
is now shunned as a contagion;
with all my people around
I am alone, a forsaken man,
a lone one with a desperate will
to drift the rudderless course
to safe shores- a vain bid;
perchance it is not worth the times,
people strangle my forlorn soul
and toll my knell in triumph.

A Form of Dirge

While the zero hour
of the cyclone-blasted hut
deadens my breath
dense drops from above
enact the nocturnal dance
as they improvise a hollow cottage
with columns of fleeting bubbles
erected on the pebbles of hailstorms;
breathless I listen
to the melting martial music
the passing away of naked minutes,
a form of dingy dirge
sprung from the bowels of the deep
filling the void of darkness.

Agony

In this unruly midnight
two stainless steel knives
full of rust to the heaving hilt
have come to grips with guilt
in lustful fury and agony;
strangely a moment ago
they cozily enjoyed
a common sheath, a slut
that did not mind the split
the sharp razing friction
and the forced tear on its wall;
The razor sharp edges
continued in mute mutiny,
nay, in loud conspiracy,
pierced through the womb
an abortive coup—an operation
Caesar is born with armour
to die on the Ides of March.

Belgium Mirror

This morn the dazed razor
gazed at my gaping face-
a hair-line cut with peeping blood
Lo! I looked straight
into the Belgium mirror
Aghast I saw my defaced face
hewn into thousand crumbs
picked up by winged cannibals;
all the hair had fled aloft
the skull transformed into bowl
beyond the hope of plastic surgery;
with insensate fury I dashed it,
all the pieces mocked at me.

The Cry

From the death cry
that pierced the heart
when the hunting arrow
nipped the neck of a dove
emerged the immortal epic;
From the agonized cry
of the oppressed brethren
crushed between the grinding
jaws of the greedy rich
ushers the drum of dissent
and the clarion of insurrection,
springs the volley of thunder bolts
and rise the potent sparks of revolt
whose flames kiss the sky
and reduce life to ashes
from which rises phoenix.

Tide

Tide
Stop thy pride
and foaming ride;
Beware
of your momentous fall
before your heart breaks
at the solid shores.

The Dark Valley

My heart bleeds, my torpid brain sizzles;
A pigmy cauldron to hold the seething riddles;
The way that used to be smooth and clear
Is now strewn with blazing sparks of fire;
The hair pricks the skull with pins of adoes,
Oh! In the veins flows the bitter gall of woes;
It saps the thought and fells the edge.
To face the shafts of life was once my pledge,
Alas! Meek suffering has become my badge
To cross the maze of misery there is no bridge,
Too many are the troubles to solve or to abridge;
Too tired of clambering up the craggy ridge
I faint and fall headlong into the vale of night
In vain I grope in the dark to catch a beam of light.

The Tedious Voyage

A tedious voyage
without destination
in dark stormy wind
gales and whales
batter the tiny boat
and tear the mast into shreds
waves rise and fall
hope and despair
dim light and darkness;
This feeling heart--
a boon or a bane?
leaves the lifeless life
in the middle of the deep sea;
Still I steer rudderless
gazing at the faint star
vainly hoping to come ashore.

I Am Tired

I am tired
in the middle of life's journey
in truth, rather crushed
betwixt the grinding jaws
of gnawing cares and disease,
echo of knell and distraction;
how many sleepless nights
shall I spend in aging agony
of uncertainty and apprehension
crowned with that eerily dark
daylight night nearly gazing at death
about to snatch my spouse away
who struggled frantically for release
fighting every moment for breath?
sitting in tears by her side
and praying the Almighty Healer
to spare her from the icy touch
lest the young ones become orphans
and frightened chicks driven
by the mighty eagle through worlds
real and unreal a ruthless race,
while my heart, transformed into cemetery,
pensively overflowed with silent songs
on the uncertainty and futility of life
as frail and momentary as a bubble;
exhausted with blasting tension
and patience consumed on the pyre of ills
my body and soul crave for quiet rest.

The Wreck

I clung to life
like a shaded ivy
or a mad lover
that adores a strumpet
but lot of filth
she flung on me
a heartless jade;
Still I am mad of her,
a doleful lover
I fear—a sad merry fear;
She my engulf me
The enchanting deluge
has already wrecked the globe
and cracked Noah's arc

My Soul in Exile

Don't quit, my love
Without you
why should I be here
and lose my identity
in this prison of a world?
How long shall I hide
this bitter potion
in my galled throat
and produce melodies
in uneasy ecstasy
with my soul in exile?
If your voice is still,
my throat doesn't move;
with glottis in pensive arrest,
tongue becomes mute
pen dry and lifeless;
Don't quit, be with me,
my prop in stress and woe
Let us sail or sink together.

A Widow

Her very sight is a sore to the mind
She is shunned as a viper
Seeing her they pause and curse
as if she is a castaway leper.
They feel her quaint breath
puts out prospect or success,
they start again in renewed joy
as they see a fox and a braying ass;
their mouths expand with tall talk
on progressive plans and reforms,
their hearts throb in lust
at her fair face at dusk
and crave to crush the jasmine
in their clenched itching fists
while her glimpse even in a mirror
transports them to heights of pleasure;
a positive word from her is a bliss
She dare not greet her own child
who has the traditional view in blood
lest the dark shadow of her gloomy fate
should fall on the newly weds!
The hunter shoots a dove in the grove
clips its wings and thrusts it in the bag
but shrinks at the sight of a forlorn widow.

An Old Woman

'Please give me alms, O charitable one!
I am an old woman with help from none' -
a familiar voice that breeds no contempt;
she lived on alms and lived near the temple gate.
Her hair as gloomily grey as clusters of snakes
unkempt, uncombed and untouched by oil
Her nails often scratched her scalp
and brutally killed lice that lived there long;
Her arms were bare with blistering boils
Her face, brow and breasts were all wrinkles
that outnumbered stitches on her soiled sari
Without a third leg her feet scarcely moved
Her eyes struggled to see with fading power
Her fingers feebly counted the coins in her bowl
A faint smile shone on her pensive face
She didn't want more than her stomach's fill
Nor did she espy the stealthy eyes of her neighbour
Still her prayers to God had a single wish
She implored Him to take her to his world sooner
She spent her laborious days for deliverance
with a beam of hope striking her heavy bosom.
The lone God was made a captive in His temple
the lone woman a victim to world's caprices;
The Swamiji saw her on his way, spat at her
and went in fury for his ill-luck to see her first.
Long back she resolved to have neither eyes nor ears.
She sat on the hard but hospitable stone for decades.
A statue of tolerance fed on ignominy
A haunting figure with a soul wrung in agony

The Corn Reaper

Under the scorching sun
in the ripened paddy field
she reaped the fallen crop
with the multi-toothed sickle;
sweat flowed drop by drop
from her care-worn brow;
the lustful eyes of the land-lord
fell on her heaving bosom;
unaware of other's eyebrow
she cut the corn patiently
sitting like a flower under the foot
thinking of her wailing child at home
and the volley of blows on her back
given last night by her drunken lord.

The Housewife

The sullen sun descends
behind the western hills
turning the land lurid and sultry;
dusk waiting like a prowling wolf
leaps and engulfs the valley
crows flap and flutter their wing
weary with bootless flying,
rest noisily on the withering boughs
of the large peepal tree
the standing sentinel of the village.
Thatched huts and walls of mud
stand as living symbols of their lifeless life.
The huge clay barrels, all empty,
emit a hollow sombre sullen smile
at the searching eyes of the housewife
who hesitates to kindle the hearth
and feeds her sunken stomach
with fond hopes of future;
She lights the cold clay lamp
with a lean burning twig
and waits with a wick in her eyes
for her partner from the furrowed field.

The Teacher

At last the gloomy day has come
After decades of devoted duty
The mind that always struggled
To transmit light to dark cavities
Is now destined to quiet decay;
Retirement from the chair or the stage
is a certainty—a worn-out truth;
it is a pensive reflection;
still man wishes time to be still
and if possible to retrace its course;
but his exit creates a vacuum;
The brassy voice is now alien to the hall
The echo haunts the mind in its fall
The receding step touches the heart
The painter paints his masterpiece
and sculptor carves his statue,
Full of life they are dumb and deaf;
but a teacher breathes life into living logs
and moulds the erring minds
into worthy beings of the species.
His guiding spirit is the pupil of his pupils
He transforms baser metal and ennobles
with the alchemic power of his word
Gift of the gab is his magic wand
that does miracles and brings metamorphosis
Teacher gives a fresh lease of life
and breathes meaning into existence;
If the Almighty creates, he re-creates
and transforms the raw substance
into a refined one, rich and noble;
Through ages he is like a candle
that burns and spreads light
ignored and forgotten after its exit.

The Snake Charmer

Squatting like a skinny skeleton
beneath a canopied tamarind tree
a lone sentinel amid a cluster of huts,
he poured breath into the gourd-pipe
which like a medieval magic wand
spread its charm of music grand
that embosomed thrill and threat;
the old and the young gazed at
the charmer and the bamboo basket;
he took off the lid restive
The cobra, the vanquished captive,
emerged like blind Samson
with a stony glitter in its lidless eyes
hissing in vain with vengeance
raising its dreaded hood
with all its mortal fangs removed;
it danced unawares in tune
with the uncanny music;
for all the risk the courted
he got a handful of rice.

My Bare Needs

Enough, enough
I want nothing
I ask nothing
They have filled
my sinking stomach
with pots of words
and my hijacked heart
with lots of promises
My hunger migrated
to the white fields
while my bare needs
get blasted by iconoclasts
My listless eyes are filled
with massive figures
of pot-bellied leaders
What more do I want?

Is the World Beautiful?

Is the world so beautiful
The rose has its thorns
Jack has its prickles,
Pandunus has its mortal asp
The rich man starves to hoard
While the beggar swallows to starve
Cattle graze the grass
and give the boon of milk
while men drink the milk
and vomit splinters of poison
and sell them to slaughter
Smiles conceal the stabs
as perfumed coffin the corpse.

In Exile

The fisherman catches fish
    with his angler
    in sea or river
The hunter or the jungleman
    kills fowl and hare
    in wood and air
        to feed
        the hungry souls
        at home
But our professed leaders
professional dissemblers
that shine in borrowed robes
in the guise of democracy
catch peoples' unlettered votes
with spurious currency notes
with lolling tongues
puffed by longing lungs
and rolling cans of toddy
ensnare and enslave human values
entrap the masses and sell their souls
auction them on the floor
of the depraved assembly;
These fleshy lying leaders
who trade in fast flesh
and relish sodden adultery
roll in smuggled comforts,
As integrity becomes crippled
hypocrisy climbs atop the ladder
and reigns supreme in seer's garb
mocking at honesty in exile.

A Search

I search
for the dark shade
beneath the sunny smiles
of blooming petals of jasmines,
for the drops of venom
that lie beneath the pot of milk,
for the sleepless tear
in the wave of evening breeze,
for the ray of constant hope
behind the halo of moonlight -
A search
to see my eye
and get my vision.

A Miracle

Don't weep my love
a tear from your eye
tears the leaf of my life
rends my heart in twain,
be unmoved of my state;
though you see
the stream of tears
flowing from my eyes
they are not tears of sorrow
they are tears of joy
pearls of peerless bliss
of our affirmed union;
you, almost a fallen leaf,
are now green and fresh;
Spring has come again
A surprise? A solace!
Or a miracle!!

Then and Now

Then
man strived
generated fire with stone
to feed and shelter his woman
he was called uncivilized;
Now
woman strives
to lit her hearth
with tearful breath
while man burns his woman
to feed his lust:
the new man of the plastic age!
As their inner selves part
she follows him to parties
as a keyed skinny doll;
A humble Eve
treading the infernal steps
of the resurrected Adam.

On the Death of Mrs. Indira Gandhi

An electric shock or a paralytic stroke
The dazzled sun ad set even at noon
'Indira is dead', nay, 'she is shot dead'
It shook the land and stunned her soul
The terrible news struck the cosy ear
With the force of Cyclop's hammer
It deadened the mind, benumbed the body
more swiftly than the heartless bullets
of a frenzied fanatic blind sten-gun
that had pierced her delicate frame
and stole the spark of her life
that lifted the land to skies of fame.

A tender creeper that blossomed
in the shady support of the big banyan
grew strong and steely in wild weather;
after the fall of the old hoary tree
it stood erect and gave shelter
under its lusty growth of leaves
to all weeds, breeds, creeds and cults
facing the stormy winds in and around;
it brought strength and dignity to the soil
unconquered by pests that tried to foil
till that fateful morn, made all mourn
when an ungrateful hand cut its span.

The beacon-light of non-aligned nations
is extinguished in a sheet of curdled blood,
The torch-bearer of disarmament summit
is borne in stately honour by pall-bearers
to the pyre at Santivan near Raj Ghat
The nightmare of her foes at home and abroad
is extinct for ever from this globe
that shone with the halo of her glow.

Gone is the light of her life
departed is the glory of the country
fled is the hope of the young elite
dead is the prop of the poor and the low.
leaving in its gory trail millions
of throbbing hearts and sobbing souls.

Democratic Lines

In this set-up of apparent democracy
a multipurpose word of lip-service
a baneful breath and an abscess,
the greater the degree of hypocrisy
the stronger the asset to be a leader;
He is masses' matinee idol
the black marketeer or the broker
the racketeer or the gambler
an unruly student to whom
academic books are untouchables
or the cine actor rolling in black money
to whom sacrifice is a strange word -
anyone can become a leader;
He knows the trick of whipping passions
which he can trade to his greedy ends
and encash the glamour to his success
a wily wolf in ass's hide reigns
a heinous hoarder in hermit's guise
strides with a load of lusty lies
content with the soaring price
of leaves and loaves, meat and rice;
As simulation becomes his element
almonds and cashew his regular aliment,
he is deaf to people's ailment;
While masses groan under his vain promises
his relatives revel in ill-gotten wealth;
the elected leader leads his caste,
the self-styled saviour saves his kindred;
A term in chair insures his progeny
from want for generations many;
Exhorting others to sacrifice gold and cash,
he liberally parts with a pinch of dusty ash;
While oppressed people await elections
he hopes to win by buying voters
with money and arrack or with posters;
If a new man comes on democratic lines
Soon he starts the game on parallel lines.

Memories

Memories are the glowing candles
that flood our journey with light
while dreams are born of desires
long cherished but hardly realized;
Days without memories and dreams
are like empty pathetic pitchers
Dreams recede but their shadows linger
Joy vanishes but its memory remains
Without yesterday, without tomorrow
today has no life nor meaning.

The Mind

Mind is the laboratory
that discloses the laws of truth
amid illusions and speculations;
it solves the insoluble
when rightly directed
for the pursuit of truth
with infinite patience.
With the spark of spirituality
it is the seat of the super-conscious;
With good discipline
it adorns the inner life
strongly steadily built
on the granite foundations
insoluble against the ages;
With the inner eye
on the everlasting and the eternal
it ignores the transitory lures;
Mind becomes rich
with an ennobling soul
the immutable image
of the supreme being.

The Kite

Behold yonder in the sky
the long-tailed eagle sailing high
drawing brittle strength
from a rain-bow twig of little length
and bonded life from a bundle of thread
a flimsy bridle to its vagaries;
It adorns the ethereal height
with its thrilling fancied flight
from the gross earthly base
as an airy messenger of peace
borne aloft on the breezy palanquin;
It comes down or gets lost
with a break in the thread
or a dent in its square space
like the unrealized dreams
of the common man;
While the upward voyage
as the flight of the winged bird
marks the soaring prices of the age
and the rising artificiality,
its steady descent embraces,
as a kite descends for a prey,
a downward trend in values;
Kite, fallen and torn on the hedge,
pensively recalls the wailing woman
molested on the sacred soil
by vultures alien to culture.

Lotus

Yonder in the pond
lotus smiles in serene joy
floating above waters
and invites to partake its bliss
and pick out pearls
from its leafy platter.
The unfolding petals
as many as the hurdles
that lie across life's journey
bloom like the blossoming soul;
It rises from the mud
but begets pure beauty
and spreads divine fragrance;
Likewise soul, encapsulated in body,
sheds slime and mortal coil,
soars to ethereal heights
and loses identity in the eternal.

Blessings of Jasmine

Jasmine flower
with its growth of pretty dower
spreading her flood of fragrance
is a divine blessing to mankind;
its soothing scent has a latent power
to enchant any in joy or sorrow;
The newly wedded couple
have their lovely whispers
beneath the jasmine bower
that scatters flowers on the pair;
they lose their sense of time
and rest on the fragrant couch.
Jasmine is soft, serene and pure
offering wondrous balm or cure
for those in woe or rapture of love
without the help of Cupid or Jove.

The Supreme Being

In the blooming petal of the flower
    I behold the smile of the Almighty
In the full blossom of the spring
    I see the fullness of the Creator
In the sonorous song of joyous birds
in the fluttering sound of their wings
in the sighs of the soft and crushed pillows
in the awesome sight of roaring billows
in the deafening sound of dark thunder
in the steady movement of the tiny beings
and in the terrible beauty of the snake
    I hear the breath of an unseen force
    formidable and inscrutable in nature;
In the midst of deep mystery around me
    I feel the grace of the Supreme Being.

Appendix 2: Reviews of *The Fleeting Bubbles*

Review by A. Russell

(A. Russel is a poet & critic based in London)

The Fleeting Bubbles is a thin sheaf of 'occasional' verses from T. Vasudeva Reddy whose love for writing poetry is a celebrated adventure in the domain of Indo-English production of our times. Should we say that he is a strong visualist often engaged in a craft to create the scene and situation where he can posit his 'poetic self' to say and to react? There is sufficient reason to believe so:

> Beneath the pale peepal tree
> by the fast-drying pond
> in that double roasted hamlet
> Woman stand like expiring candles.

Image-packed a scene is built up with little strain and some felicity; only that his syntax is a bit strained, phrasing no less laboured. The import of his lines comes off; straight away he gives away without any attempt of concealing what he needs to state. So by the time you are at the last line you can walk off with the bloc of sensibility inscribed into your psyche.

In short poems where the statement dominates, rather constituting the nucleus, what he says is given a poetry form, clarity becomes grace, and no lapses in craft can mar the art of being genuine and frank about one's feelings. The control over syntax is commendable if not perfect.

> I fled from you, from me and all
> I thought so, but alas!
> I found myself amid you
> like a frightened cat.

Stock images do not sound jaded in such situations; even they acquire edge, the ability to encapsulate feelings. In 'Agony' he is poignant and phrases are composed to a rare control. A remarkable feature of his self exposition is that he is not sentimental anywhere.

'I am tired' is a self-exploration that rises to an acme of pathos without being self-indulgent or pathetic. He keeps his prose by tightening up the structure sprucely composed, some poems reveal that he has trained his mind on saying things in a poetic fashion. Even the jejune sound interesting and the drably familiar acquires a halo of mystery.

Though he writes in English he does not anglicize his thoughts. Nor does he hide his emotions as the pseudo-English so often do in the worn-out fashion of neo-metaphysicals. He remains a native, an Indian in what he thinks about the world in its enigmatic appeal, a pantheist at the core of his heart. His is stuff with a distinctly Indian flavour, the ripe jackfruit and appetizing yellow of mango in a basket.

(Published in *Poetry Time*, No. 1 & 2, 1990)

Review by Dr. Rosemary C. Wilkinson

(Secretary General, World Poetry Society Intercontinental, San Francisco)

I read your new book *The Fleeting Bubbles* listening to Mozart. How you are gifted! Each poem leads us into the soul of India—into the roadway that I travelled while in the South of India. It brings so much back to me all over again. The people come alive, the trees bemoan their burden under the hot sun and you touch the reader with a beautiful cadence and natural rhyme.

In 'The Cry' we experience the very death taking place and uplifted at the closing reminding of our ashes which will again rise like the phoenix:

> From the agonized cry
> of the oppressed brethren
> crushed between the grinding
> jaws of the greedy rich
> ushers the drum of dissent
> and the clarion of insurrection,
> springs the volley of thunder bolts
> and rise the potent sparks of revolt
> whose flames kiss the sky
> and reduce life to ashes
> from which rises phoenix. (*Fleeting Bubbles*, p.13)

Your choice of words to describe 'The Dark Valley' strikes like the flash of a lightning even though "In vain you grope in the dark to catch a beam of light." My ear wants to listen to this poem over and over again and the natural rhyme beckons me to hear it over and over. When all the world seems to be breaking we want to lament with you knowing how true it all is!

> Too many are the troubles to solve or to abridge,
> Too tired of clambering up the craggy ridge
> I faint and fall headlong into the vale of night
> In vain I grope in the dark to catch a beam of light.
> (p.15)

'The House Wife' is especially poignant, for so many do not have that luxury today but drawn away from home, children, to make mortgage payments to have roof over their heads:

> Dusk waiting like a prowling wolf
> leaps and engulfs the valley
> Crows flap and flutter their wing
> weary with bootless flying,
> rest noisily on the withering boughs
> of the large peepal tree
> the standing sentinel of the village;
> Thatched huts and walls of mud
> stand as living symbols of their lifeless life.
> ..... She lights the clay lamp
> with a burning twig
> and waits with a wick in her eyes
> for her partner from the furrowed field. (p.23)

At this time in history, the family roots are being cut down more and more. Hence the highest divorce rates, the highest re-marriages, the highest suicides, the highest abortions, the highest teen-age marriages because of the sexual revolution, the highest drop-outs in high school, and now children who know whole sets of new relations because of multiple marriages and of course couples living together rearing children without marriage. So to read this book is to live in all the values we knew traditionally on a firm basis and now we know why you titled your book as *The Fleeting Bubbles*. All our vagaries and vanities and pleasures are in fact fleeting bubbles. Our life itself is a fleeting bubble! The book ends on a right note with the poem 'Supreme Being' which indeed a supreme jewel glowing with sublime light. Our solace comes from the mind and heart whereby we retreat closer and closer to God—He alone gives us peace, to withstand it all.

Congratulations for this new book. I pray you continue to bring out your important work and that it will be read the world over, for its message is universal.

(Her letter dated Aug.,1989.)

Review by Prof. Sankarasan Parida

'The Fleeting Bubbles' is definitely a great contribution to modern Indo-Anglian poetry. All the 39 poems are impregnated with stimulating fervours distracted and deduced out of a wide variety of experiences and perceptive calibre and personal feelings in various situations. The rhythm in his lyrical lines is at once touching and invigorating even the mute psychic state. The striking images and structure of lucid lines tinged with imagination created wonderful results. His deep insight in life and nature makes him aware of the magnificent sights which he bursts out most successfully so as attract the attention of all poetry lovers. Sometimes he is satirical and ironical of the injustice going on in various spheres in the Society.

The village women bringing water from the pond are like "famished cattle that drain water to the lees". The Indian bride in the poem of the same title is

> "Dressed in gold-laced Kanchi silk sari
> adorned with stone-studded jewellery
> she looks like a bedecked doll in a showcase
> or a vanishing species in a zoo".

The influence of John Keats is felt in the poem 'When I churned Time':

> "Bubbles of heart aches
> sprang spasmodically"

and Keats writes,

> "My heart aches
> A drowsy numbness pains my sense".
>
> (Ode to Nightingale)

The poem 'Flux of life' is replete with the tone of T.S.Eliot; Dr. Reddy writes,

> We should have some work
> to distract us from distraction".

T.S. Eliot writes, "We are distracted from distraction by distraction". Poems like 'A Form of Dirge', 'Agony' 'Belgium Mirror', 'In Tense Flight', 'The Cry', 'Tide', 'I am Tired', 'My Soul in Exile', etc are extremely touching and thought –provoking. These poems explicate certain aspects of human life which spring from a profound sense of observation of different facets and now the poet wants rest, 'My body and soul crave for quiet rest".

The spectacular delineation of the life of an old woman startles any sensitive reader.

> Her nails often scratched her scalp
> And brutally killed lice that lived there long" (An Old Woman)

The form and content are beautifully blended in it—

> "The lone God was made a captive in His temple
> The lone woman a victim to world's caprices".

While going through 'The Corn Reaper' one is reminded of 'The Solitary Reaper' of Wordsworth. In both cases there is sorrow and suffering but in a different way. Look at the lines of Dr. Reddy:

> she cut the corn patiently Sitting
> like a flower under the foot
> thinking of her wailing child at home
> and the volley of blows on her back
> given last night by her drunken lord. (p.22)

In 'The Teacher' the poet is taking us to a naked truth.

> Through ages he is like a candle
> that burns and spreads light
> ignored and forgotten after its extinction"

'In Exile' is a beautiful critique on modern politicians. The heart-rending experience at the sad and sudden death of Mrs. Indira Gandhi stirs the poet and he bursts out with some startling lines in "On the death of Mrs. Indira Gandhi".

The readers are feasted with some fine bread of intellectual pursuit and pensiveness while going through 'Memories', 'The Mind', 'The Kite', 'Lotus', and 'The Supreme Being'. The anthology has a variety of concerns touching the brims of numerous situations and circumstances so as to stir and stimulate the reader both in its themes and treatment.

(Published in *POETCRIT*, Jan. 1990)

Review by Dr. D.C. Chambial

(D.C. Chambial is a Poet, Critic & Editor, *Poetcrit*)

Dr. T. Vasudeva Reddy, a well-known name in the domain of Indian English poetry, has already secured a place of prominence. His two earlier volumes of poetry are *When Grief Rains*, and *Broken Rhythms*. About his creativity A. Russell has rightly remarked, "..the variety of themes bear a testimony to the fertility of his creative perception." His poems have also been translated into French.

He is a poet of the masses. In these poems we come across the unending suffering, that has compelled the attention of the modern humanists. His poem 'An Old Woman' describes a beggar woman in concrete imagery:

> A statue of tolerance fed on ignominy
> A haunting figure with a soul wrung in agony (p.21).

A widow is considered ill ominous. A mere sight of her before starting anything initiates people to curse her. She cannot even welcome her newly wedded son:

> She dare not greet her own child
> who has the traditional view in blood
> lest the dark shadow of her gloomy fate
> should fall on the newly weds! (p.20).

Here he gives an expression to an orthodox view held by our society preventing a widow share any joy. In 'The Snake Charmer' who takes the risk of catching poisonous cobra and charming people with his (cobra's) dance. The poet sympathizes with him and writes:

> For all the risk he courted
> he got a handful of rice" (p.2).

'Then and Now' presents a beautiful contrast of values of the uncivilized man of pre-historic age with the civilized man of modern age: "Then/man strived/generated fire with stone/to feed and shelter his woman/...Now/ woman strives/ to lit her hearth/ with tearful breath/ while man burns his woman/ to feed his lust;"(p.31) Who is more civilized?

His philosophical outlook on life also brings out suffering; in 'When I Churned Time' he cogitates:

> my nebulous experience....
> sprang spasmodically/precipitating into

> a potful of bitter potion
> incarnating into mitral stenosis
> that made me gasp for breath
> I am no Lord Shiva
> to swallow the *halahala*;

and in 'The Dark Valley' he avers: "To face the shafts of life was once my pledge./Alas! meek suffering has become my badge." (p.15) 'Tide' is a short wonderful lyric full of movement and warning against the false pride:

> Tide
> stop thy pride
> and foaming ride
> Beware
> of your momentous fall
> before your heart breaks
> at the solid shores" (p.14).

He implores his soul not to desert him. Here is the illustration: "Don't quit; be with me/ my prop in stress and woe/Let us sail or sink together." (p.19). His metaphysical mind finds God in everything in his poem 'The Supreme Being':

> In the deep mystery around me
> I feel the grace of the Supreme Being (p.39)

In his poem 'The Indian Bride' he makes a satirical dig at the social evil of dowry:

> the triple knot of *thali* around her neck
> shining symbol of new bondage
> mocks at the thrice cursed bride
> Having bought the groom in auction
> as cattle dealers buy their lusty bulls   (p.2).

In the same vein he satirizes senior doctors "in white robes/ behave like white elephants./ A few new-hatched doctors/wear airs pruning their plumage like young Chanticleers" (p.3). He very piquantly and accurately paints the hapless picture of the poor corn reaper in the poem entitled 'The Corn Reaper':

> she cut the corn patiently
> sitting like a flower under the foot
> thinking of her waiting child at home

> and of the volley of blows on her back
> given last night by her drunken lord   (p.22).

His use of transferred epithet: 'uncanny music', 'sunny smiles', 'sullen sun', 'fond hopes'; similes—

> Days without memories and dreams
> are like empty pitchers' (p.34),

and "she is shunned as a viper!' (p.20) suggest something more than what is said. Corrupt politicians and hoarders do not escape his scathing pen. In this volume he has emerged as a potent poet rooted deep in the soil from where many young poets may learn how to furrow field and sow seeds of lovely lyrics rich in socio-politico-cultural consciousness.

(published in *Canopy,* Sept.1993, pp. 38-39)

About the Commentator

Born in 1947 Ramesh Chandra Mukhopadhyaya M A (Triple) MPhil, PhD is a retired college teacher now residing at 6/1 Amrita Lal Nath Lane, P O Belur Math, Howrah, West Bengal, India, Pin 711202. A Bilingual writer (English and Bengali), he has been writing on different subjects for the last thirty years. He seeks to retrieve the wealth of poetry when it is a revelation. Dr. Mukhopadhyaya regards K. V. Dominic as a poet of a seer.

Dr Mukhopadhyaya is a soldier of the Underground Poetry Movement in present day Bengali literature. His Decoding *Hidden Face Flower*, a collection of *explicatio de texte* of the avant garde Vietnamese poet Mai Van Phan has been published by the Publishing House of Vietnams Writers Association in 2015. Dr Mukhopdhyaya has been awarded Ashutosh Mukherjee gold medal for writing a treatise on modern Bengali drama.

About the Author

Dr. T. Vasudeva Reddy, born in Dec. 1943 in a village near the famous pilgrim town Tirupati in Andhra State in India, did M.A in English in 1966 and got Ph. D. for his thesis on the novels of Jane Austen. He worked as Lecturer, Reader and U.G.C National Fellow and Visiting Professor, and retired as Principal of Govt. Degree College in Dec. 2001 and later as Principal of prestigious Post-Graduate colleges. He received the Awards of International Eminent Poet in 1987, Hon. D. Litt. from the WAAC, San Francisco in 1988, Best Teacher Award at the College & University level from the Govt. of A.P. in 1990, Best Poetry award for his third poetry book *The Fleeting Bubbles* from Michael Madhusudan Dutt Academy, Calcutta in 1994 and the prestigious U.G.C Award of National Fellowship in 1998. His biography figures in the American Biographical Institute (N. Carolina, USA), International Biographical Institute (Cambridge), Reference India & Asia (New Delhi) and Sahitya Akademi (New Delhi).

He is a renowned poet, critic and novelist of international repute. His poems appeared in French journals in Paris. M.Phil. and Ph.D. theses have been produced on his works. He received the international Award of "Excellence in World Poetry" in 2009. He is now Hon. President of GIEWEC (Guild of Indian English Writers Editors and Critics). He is an internationally recognized poet in English with 11 poetry books to his credit. His poetic career spans over a long period of three and a half decades from 1982 till now and his creative quill knows no rest. He is at once a realistic and romantic poet, a lover of nature and a poet with social commitment, a lyricist and a satirist aiming at the improvement of ethical standards.

As Prof. David Kerr of Monash Univ. Australia says, "T.V. Reddy is a real poet with a commitment to perfection....His poetry is an outburst of emotion and it succeeds in creating the basic human feelings." In the words of Prof. Nissim Ezekiel, a distinguished Indian poet, "Like a gifted sculptor he chisels his poems with the deftness of a master craftsman."

Other Works by T.V. Reddy

Poetry:
When Grief Rains (New Delhi, Samakaleen Pubs., 1982)
The Broken Rhythms (Madras, Poets Press, 1987)
The Fleeting Bubbles (Madras, Poets Press, 1989)
*Melting Melodies (*Madras, Poets Press, 1994)
Pensive Memories (Madras, Poets Press, 2005)
Gliding Ripples (U.S.A., Baltimore, Pub. America, 2008)
Echoes (N. Delhi, Authors Press, 2012)
Quest for Peace (N. Delhi, Authors Press, 2013)
Golden Veil (N. Delhi, Authors Press, 2016)
Thousand Haiku Pearls (N. Delhi, Authors Press, 2016)
Sound and Silence (N.Delhi, Authors Press, 2017)
The Rural Muse: The Poetry of T. Vasudeva Reddy. Ed. K.V. Raghupathi (N. Delhi, Authors Press, 2014).

Novels:
The Vultures (Calcutta, Golden Books, 1983)
Minor Gods (New York, 2008)

Criticism:
Jane Austen: The Dialectics of Self-Actualization in her Novels (New Delhi, Sterling Pubs., 1987)
Jane Austen: The Matrix of Matrimony (Jaipur, Bohra Pubs., 1987)
A Critical Survey of Indo-English Poetry (N. Delhi, Authors Press, 2016).

Grammar:
Advanced Grammar & Composition in English (Hyderabad, Commonwealth Pubs., 1996)

Index

A

A Form of Dirge, 100
Agony, 79–81, 80
    text, 126
Andhra, 163

B

banyan tree, 10, 66
Belgium Mirror, 81–83
Belguim Mirror
    text, 127
Bhagavad Gita, 10, 51, 83, 99, 102, 108
Birth Day Party, 40–43
    text, 120
Blessings of Jasmine
    text, 148
Brahmasutra, 104
Broken Rhythms, 5, 113, 157, 164

C

Caesar, 80, 100, 126
Corn Reaper, The, 29–31
    text, 136
Cry, The, 64–65, 90
    text, 128

D

Dark Lady, 94, 95
Dark Valley, The, 75, 101, 153, 158
    text, 129
Delphi, 47, 48
Democratic Lines, 54–58, 58, 60, 66, 90, 91, 101, 103
    text, 145
Dhammapada, 108
Dharma, S., 101
Duryodhana, 91, 92
Dutt, T., iii, iv, 1, 2, 163

E

Eliot, T.S., 11, 41, 77, 84, 85, 155
Endymion, 102
Exile, 54–58
Ezekiel, N., 9, 163

F

Flux of Life, 100
    text, 124
Forlorn Soul, A., 74, 75, 77, 94
    text, 125
Form of Dirge, A., 63–64
    text, 126
Friedenkraft, G., 113–14

G

GIEWEC, 163

H

Hospital, The, 43–50, 73, 99
    text, 119
House Wife, The, 31–32, 153
Housewife, The
    text, 137

I

I Am Tired, 73, 76, 99
    text, 131
In Exile, 55, 57, 58, 90, 92, 93, 101, 156
    text, 141
In Tense Flight, 78

text, 123
Indian Bride, The, 14–23
   text, 118
Is the World Beautiful?, 103
   text, 140

K

kalash, 11
Kaleswar, 100
Kalidasa, 1
Kerr, D., 163
Kite, The, 66–69
   text, 147
krauncha, 64
Kumar, S.K., 9

L

Let the Eyes Be Shut, 50–52
   text, 122
Lok Sabha, 56
Lord Rama, 65, 108
Lord Siva, 70, 74, 75, 100, 103, 121
Lotus, 102, 109
   text, 148

M

Mahabharata, The, 1, 3, 91
Memories, 81, 86, 101
   text, 146
Mephistopheles, 49, 54
Milton, 34, 54, 76
Mind, The, 97, 101
   text, 146
Miracle, A., 39, 87, 104
   text, 142
mitral stenosis, 69, 70, 84, 158
My Bare Needs, 61–63, 91
   text, 140
My Soul in Exile, 86, 87, 98
   text, 133
My Soul's Agony, 77

N

Naidu, S., 1, 2

O

Old Woman, An, 27–29, 97, 113, 156, 157
   text, 135
On the Death of Mrs. Indira Gandhi, 65–66, 144

P

Paramatma, 102
Parthasarathy, R., 3
Pensive Memories, 5, 164
Peripeteia, 49
Pope, A., 57
Pythia, 47, 48

Q

Quixote, Don, 49

R

Raghuvamsam, 46
Reddy, C.R., 2–3
Rossetti, D.G., 15, 110

S

Samson, 34, 139
Search, A, 74, 103
   text, 142
Shakespeare, 1, 6, 76, 82, 94, 95, 103
Shelley, 1, 31, 63, 64, 67, 76, 90
Snake Charmer, The, 33–35, 93, 157
   text, 139
Srinivas, K., 4, 5
Supreme Being, The, 99, 105, 110, 111, 114, 156, 158
   text, 149

T

Tamburlaine, 46, 63
Teacher, The, 58–61, 80
   text, 138
Tedious Voyage, The, 75, 101, 103, 104
   text, 130
Thanatos, 27, 49, 75
The Wreck, 94
Then and Now, 37–40, 38, 101, 157

text, 143
Tide
  text, 128
Tirupati, 163

U

Underground Literature Movement, iii
Upanishads, 82, 99, 105, 110, 111

V

Valmiki, 1, 64, 65, 70, 89, 107, 108
Vyasa, 1

W

When Grief Rains, 4, 77, 113, 157, 164
When I Churned Time, 69–71, 75, 80, 84, 100, 157
  text, 121
Widow, A, 23–27
  text, 134
Women of the Village, 10–14, 99
  text, 117
Wordsworth, 1, 29, 30, 31, 61, 67, 97, 110, 156
Wreck, The, 94
  text, 132

Y

Yahovah, 42

The Pulse of Life: Essential Readings is a representative collection of the poetry of T. Vasudeva Reddy, a luminous star shining in Indian English poetry. His poetry is a pleasant blend of the traditional and the modern, the realistic and the romantic, the symbolic and the imagist, the urban and the rural, satirical and lyrical streams of poetry. His poems cover a wide thematic pattern ranging from the remote village to the global level, a bewildering blend of rural and global life. Whoever wishes to have a glimpse of the reality of the Indian rural scenario and see the struggles and sufferings of poor farmers can go through the poems of T.V. Reddy. Poems, spread over eleven volumes till now, and spanning 35 years, are now collected for the first time ever in this Essential Readings edition.

"In the vast desert of Indo-Anglian poetry, it is quite refreshing to see the life-giving oasis of Reddi's poetry which at once resuscitates and invigorates even a slumbering mind. His poems are as immortal as the frescoes of the famous Ajantha caves in India."

--Dr. Edith Rusconi Kaltovich, N.J.

"My attention is sometimes arrested by the striking imagery and phrasing. The poet has a keen eye to mark the exceptional whether in life or nature."

--Dr. K.R. Srinivas Iyengar, Madras

"In his poetry we find concrete examples of poetic excellences that distinguish him from other Indian poets and reserve for him a permanent place on the Indian Parnassus. Every poem is a nugget of thoughtful fancy studded in the fabric of the poet's pageant of poetic filigree."

--Dr. D.C. Chambial, Editor, *Poetcrit*, H.P.

From Modern History Press
www.ModernHistoryPress.com

Join us on a poetic journey to the soul of India

The Poetry of T.V. Reddy is grounded in human struggles and unrest, social as well as psychological and depicts the varied shades of restlessness that is the order of modern times. He protests against the social ills and evils in a gripping way in his absorbing poetry. He paints his experiences in a characteristic choice diction and the different images that he has carved out of human life and nature make a deep impression on the minds of the readers and linger there. The poet takes the readers into the soul of India, the villages and rural life which are the backbone of the country—that speaks volumes of his commitment to rural element and makes people come alive in his poetry. Natural rhyme and rhythm of the poems creates the pleasing melody. Clarity of thought and lucidity of expression, splendid imagery and marvelous melody are the hallmarks of his poetry.

-- Dr. P.V. Laxmiprasad, Editor

T.V. Reddy is not only a poet of highly perceptive temperament but also an accomplished critic and novelist. His awesome ingenious insight into the purpose and meaning of life in a perceptive and intuitive way leads the reader to the invisible force meticulously driving the point that the spiritual region lying within a man offers solace, harmony and consolation par excellence. For Reddy often finds strong affinity in Indian soil and here, rural backdrop inspires him to cultivate niceties of life where rural-oriented background turns out religious for him.

-- P.C.K. Prem, Authoritative critic on Indian English Poetry from Himachal Paradesh, India

From Modern History Press
www.ModernHistoryPress.com

www.ingramcontent.com/pod-product-compliance
Lightning Source LLC
Chambersburg PA
CBHW071204160426
43196CB00011B/2198